AF894946

Microsoft® Internet Explorer 5

Illustrated Essentials

Jessica Evans

COURSE TECHNOLOGY
Thomson Learning™
ONE MAIN STREET, CAMBRIDGE, MA 02142

Australia • Canada • Denmark • Japan • Mexico • New Zealand • Philippines
Puerto Rico • Singapore • South Africa • Spain • United Kingdom • United States

Microsoft Internet Explorer 5—Illustrated Essentials is published by Course Technology

Senior Product Manager:	Kathryn Schooling
Product Manager:	Jennifer A. Duffy
Associate Product Manager:	Emily Heberlein
Contributing Authors:	Ann Barron, Chet Lyskawa, Sasha Vodnik
Production Editor:	Ellina Beletsky
Developmental Editor:	Janice Jutras
Marketing Manager:	Karen Bartlett
Editorial Assistant:	Stacie Parillo
Composition House:	GEX, Inc.
QA Manuscript Reviewers:	Jeff Schwartz, Alex White
Text Designer:	Joseph Lee, Joseph Lee Designs
Cover Designer:	Doug Goodman, Doug Goodman Designs

For more information contact:

Course Technology
One Main Street
Cambridge, MA 02142

Or find us on the Word Wide Web at: www.course.com

Disclaimer

ISBN 0-7600-6147-5

Printed in the United States of America

1 2 3 4 5 6 7 8 9 BM 04 03 02 01 00

The Illustrated Series Offers the Entire Package for your Microsoft Office 2000 Needs

Office 2000 MOUS Certification Coverage

The Illustrated Series offers a growing number of Microsoft-approved titles that cover the objectives required to pass the Office 2000 MOUS (Microsoft Office User Specialist) exams. After studying with any of the approved Illustrated titles, you will have mastered the Core and Expert skills necessary to pass any Office 2000 MOUS exam.

Helpful New Features

The Illustrated Series responded to customer feedback by changing the red font in the Steps to green for easier reading, and adding new conceptual lessons to units to give students the extra information they need when learning Office 2000.

New Exciting Case and Innovative On-Line Companion

There is an exciting new case study used throughout our textbooks, a fictitious chain of bookstore cafés called MediaLoft, designed to be "real-world" in nature by introducing the kinds of activities that students will encounter when working with Microsoft Office 2000. The **MediaLoft Web site**, available at www.course.com/illustrated/medialoft, mirrors the case study used throughout the book, creating a real-world intranet site that the fictional employees of MediaLoft would use for communication and collaboration on projects. This Companion is used to complete the WebWorks exercise in each unit of this book, and to allow students to become familiar with the business application of an intranet site.

Enhance Any Illustrated Text with these Exciting Products!

Course CBT

Enhance your students' Office 2000 classroom learning experience with self-paced computer-based training on CD-ROM. Course CBT engages students with interactive multimedia and hands-on simulations that reinforce and complement the concepts and skills covered in the textbook. All the content is aligned with the MOUS program, making it a great preparation tool for the certification exams. Course CBT also includes extensive pre- and post-assessments that test students' mastery of skills.

Course Assessment

How well do your students *really* know Microsoft Office? Course Assessment is a performance-based testing program that measures students' proficiency in Microsoft Office 2000. Previously known as SAM, Course Assessment is available for Office 2000 in either a live or simulated environment. You can use Course Assessment to place students into or out of courses, monitor their performance throughout a course, and help prepare them for the MOUS certification exams.

Create Your Ideal Course Package with CourseKits™

If one book doesn't offer all the coverage you need, create a course package that does. With Course Technology's CourseKits—our mix-and-match approach to selecting texts—you have the freedom to combine products from more than one series. When you choose any two or more Course Technology products for one course, we'll discount the price and package them together so your students can pick up one convenient bundle at the bookstore.

For more information about any of these offerings or other Course Technology products, contact your sales representative or visit our web site at:

www.course.com

Preface

Welcome to *Microsoft Internet Explorer 5—Illustrated Essentials.* This highly visual book offers users a hands-on introduction to basic aspects of Microsoft Internet Explorer 5 and also serves as an excellent reference for future use. If you would like additional coverage of Microsoft Internet Explorer 5, we also offer *The World Wide Web featuring Microsoft Internet Explorer 5—Illustrated Introductory.*

▶ Organization and Coverage

This text contains two units that cover basic skills. In these units, students learn how to use Internet Explorer 5 to browse the Web. Students also learn how to plan and create a Web document using other Office applications, and add hyperlinks.

▶ About this Approach

What makes the Illustrated approach so effective at teaching software skills? It's quite simple. Each skill is presented on two facing pages, with the step-by-step instructions on the left page, and large screen illustrations on the right. Students can focus on a single skill without having to turn the page. This unique design makes information extremely accessible and easy to absorb, and provides a great reference for after the course is over. This hands-on approach also makes it ideal for both self-paced or instructor-led classes.

Each lesson, or "information display," contains the following elements:

Each 2-page spread focuses on a single skill.

Clear step-by-step directions explain how to complete the specific task, with what students are to type in green. When students follow the numbered steps, they quickly learn how each procedure is performed and what the results will be.

Concise text that introduces the basic principles discussed in the lesson. Procedures are easier to learn when concepts fit into a framework.

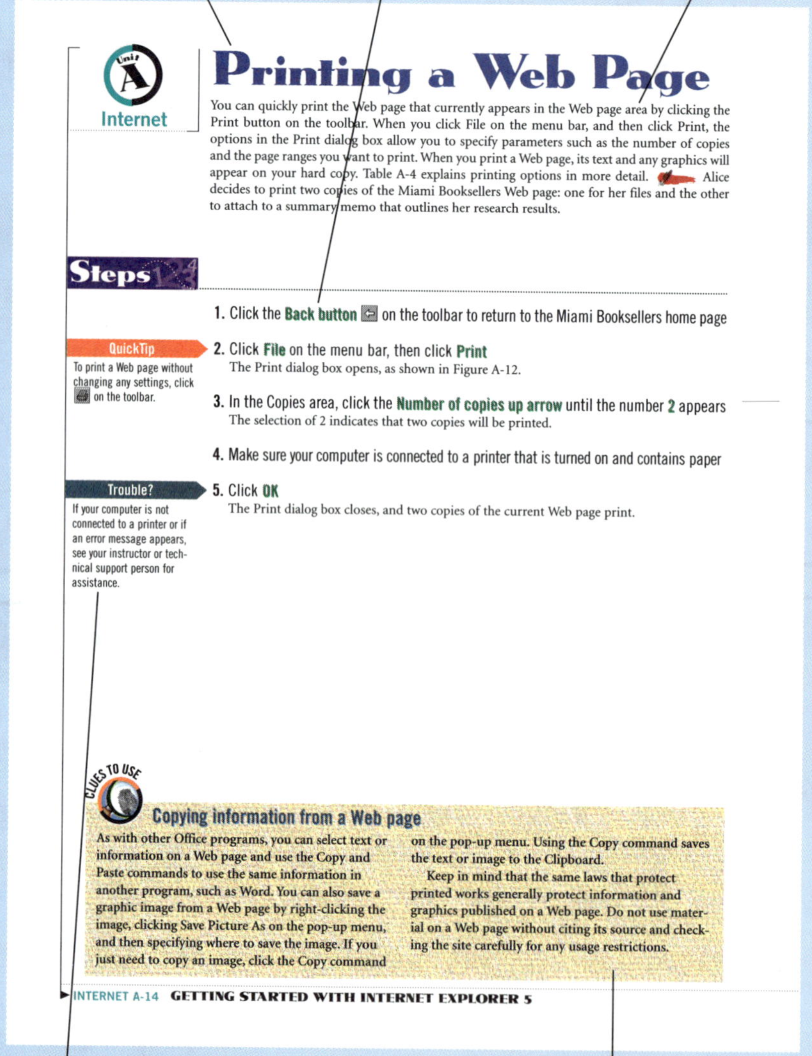

Unit A Internet

Printing a Web Page

You can quickly print the Web page that currently appears in the Web page area by clicking the Print button on the toolbar. When you click File on the menu bar, and then click Print, the options in the Print dialog box allow you to specify parameters such as the number of copies and the page ranges you want to print. When you print a Web page, its text and any graphics will appear on your hard copy. Table A-4 explains printing options in more detail. Alice decides to print two copies of the Miami Booksellers Web page: one for her files and the other to attach to a summary memo that outlines her research results.

Steps

1. Click the **Back button** on the toolbar to return to the Miami Booksellers home page
2. Click **File** on the menu bar, then click **Print**
   The Print dialog box opens, as shown in Figure A-12.
3. In the Copies area, click the **Number of copies up arrow** until the number **2** appears
   The selection of 2 indicates that two copies will be printed.
4. Make sure your computer is connected to a printer that is turned on and contains paper
5. Click **OK**
   The Print dialog box closes, and two copies of the current Web page print.

QuickTip
To print a Web page without changing any settings, click on the toolbar.

Trouble?
If your computer is not connected to a printer or if an error message appears, see your instructor or technical support person for assistance.

Clues to Use

Copying information from a Web page

As with other Office programs, you can select text or information on a Web page and use the Copy and Paste commands to use the same information in another program, such as Word. You can also save a graphic image from a Web page by right-clicking the image, clicking Save Picture As on the pop-up menu, and then specifying where to save the image. If you just need to copy an image, click the Copy command on the pop-up menu. Using the Copy command saves the text or image to the Clipboard.

Keep in mind that the same laws that protect printed works generally protect information and graphics published on a Web page. Do not use material on a Web page without citing its source and checking the site carefully for any usage restrictions.

INTERNET A-14 GETTING STARTED WITH INTERNET EXPLORER 5

Hints as well as trouble-shooting advice, right where you need it – next to the step itself.

Clues to Use boxes provide concise information that either expands on one component of the major lesson skill or describes an independent task that is in some way related to the major lesson skill.

Every lesson features large-size, full-color representations of what the students' screen should look like after completing the numbered steps.

FIGURE A-12: Print dialog box

Your printer information might differ

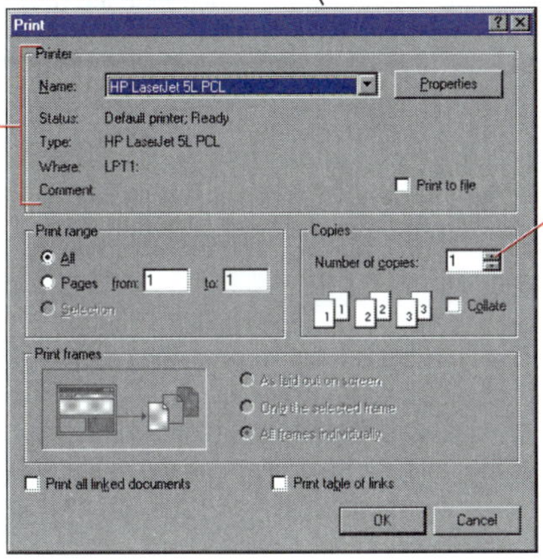

Click to increase number of copies

TABLE A-4: Printing options

option	description
Printer	Displays information about the name, status, type, and location of the active printer
Properties	Allows you to specify parameters such as paper size, paper source, and orientation
Print range	Allows you to choose to print all pages, a range of pages, or a selection on a page
Copies	Indicates the number of copies of each page to print and their sequence
Print frames	Allows you to print only the current frame or all frames separately or together
Print all linked documents	Opens and prints each document referenced by a link on the current page
Print table of links	Prints links in a table at the end of the document

Internet

GETTING STARTED WITH INTERNET EXPLORER 5 INTERNET A-15

Quickly accessible summaries of key terms, toolbar buttons, or keyboard alternatives connected with the lesson material. Students can refer easily to this information when working on their own projects at a later time.

The page numbers are designed like a road map. Internet indicates the Internet section, A indicates the first unit, and 15 indicates the page within the unit.

Other Features

The two-page lesson format featured in this book provides the new user with a powerful learning experience. Additionally, this book contains the following features:

► Real-World Case

The case study used throughout the textbook, a fictitious company called MediaLoft, is designed to be "'real-world" in nature and introduces the kinds of activities that students will encounter when working with Internet Explorer 5. With a real-world case, the process of solving problems will be more meaningful to students.

Students can also enhance their skills by completing the Web Works exercises in each unit by going to the innovative Student Online Companion, available at **www.course.com/illustrated/medialoft**. The MediaLoft site mirrors the case study by acting as the company's intranet site, further allowing students to become familiar with applicable business scenarios.

► End of Unit Material

Each unit concludes with a Concepts Review that tests students' understanding of what they learned in the unit. The Concepts Review is followed by a Skills Review, which provides students with additional hands-on practice of the skills. The Skills Review is followed by Independent Challenges, which pose case problems for students to solve. At least one Independent Challenge in each unit asks students to use the World Wide Web to solve the problem as indicated by a Web Work icon. The Visual Workshops that follow the Independent Challenges help students develop critical thinking skills. Students are shown completed Web pages or screens and are asked to recreate them.

Instructor's Resource Kit

The Instructor's Resource Kit is Course Technology's way of putting the resources and information needed to teach and learn effectively into your hands. With an integrated array of teaching and learning tools that offers you and your students a broad range of technology-based instructional options, we believe this kit represents the highest quality and most cutting edge resources available to instructors today. Many of these resources are available at www.course.com. The resources available with this book are:

MediaLoft Web site Available at **www.course.com/illustrated/medialoft**, this innovative Student Online Companion enhances and augments the printed page by bringing students onto the Web for a dynamic and continually updated learning experience. The MediaLoft site mirrors the case study used throughout the book, creating a real-world intranet site for this fictitious company, a national chain of bookstore cafés. This Companion is used to complete the WebWorks exercise in each unit of this book, and to allow students to become familiar with the business application of an intranet site.

Instructor's Manual Available as an electronic file, the Instructor's Manual is quality-assurance tested and includes unit overviews, project file listing, detailed lecture topics for each unit with teaching tips, an Upgrader's Guide, solutions to all lessons and end-of-unit material, and extra Independent Challenges. The Instructor's Manual is available on the Instructor's Resource Kit CD-ROM, or you can download it from **www.course.com**.

Course Faculty Online Companion You can browse this textbook's password-protected site to obtain the Instructor's Manual, Solution Files, Project Files, and any updates to the text. Contact your Customer Service Representative for the site address and password.

Project Files Project Files contain all of the data that students will use to complete the lessons and end-of-unit material. A Readme file includes instructions for using the files. Adopters of this text are granted the right to install the Project Files on any standalone computer or network. The Project Files are available on the Instructor's Resource Kit CD-ROM, the Review Pack, and can also be downloaded from www.course.com.

Solution Files Solution Files contain every file students are asked to create or modify in the lessons and end-of-unit material. A Help file on the Instructor's Resource Kit includes information for using the Solution Files.

Course Test Manager Designed by Course Technology, this Windows-based testing software helps instructors design, administer, and print tests and pre-tests. A full-featured program, Course Test Manager also has an online testing component that allows students to take tests at the computer and have their exams automatically graded.

Figure Files The figures in the text are provided on the Instructor's Resource Kit CD-ROM to help illustrate key topics or concepts. Instructors can create traditional overhead transparencies by printing the figure files, or they can create electronic slide shows by using the figures in a presentation program such as PowerPoint.

WebCT WebCT is a tool used to create Web-based educational environments and also uses WWW browsers as the interface for the course-building environment. The site is hosted on your school campus, allowing complete control over the information. WebCT has its own internal communication system, offering internal e-mail, a Bulletin Board, and a Chat room.

Course Technology offers pre-existing supplemental information to help in your WebCT class creation, such as a suggested Syllabus, Lecture Notes, Figures in the Book / Course Presenter, Student Downloads, and Test Banks in which you can schedule an exam, create reports, and more.

Contents

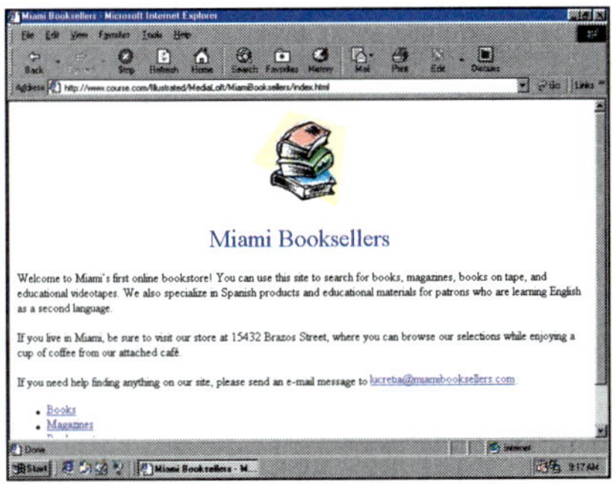

Contents

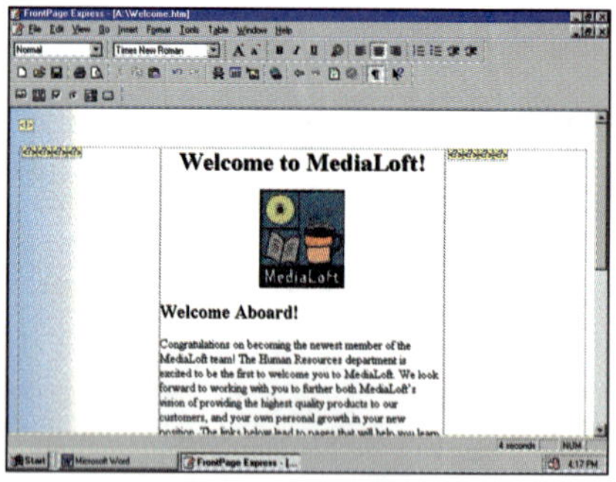

Internet

Unit A

Getting Started with Internet Explorer 5

Objectives

- Understand Web browsers
- Start Internet Explorer
- Explore the browser window
- Open and save a URL
- Navigate Web pages
- Get Help
- Print a Web page
- Search for information on the Internet
- Exit Internet Explorer

In this unit, you learn how to use the World Wide Web, examine basic features of Internet Explorer 5, and access Web pages. You need to connect to the Internet to complete this unit. If your computer is not connected to the Internet, check with your instructor or technical support person to get connected, or, if necessary, simply read the lessons without completing the steps to learn about using Internet Explorer. MediaLoft is a chain of café bookstores founded in 1988. MediaLoft stores offer customers the opportunity to purchase books, music, and videotapes while enjoying a variety of exotic coffees, teas, and freshly baked desserts. Alice Wegman is the marketing manager at MediaLoft. Alice needs to determine if MediaLoft should continue its nationwide expansion by opening a store in southern Florida. She decides to use Internet Explorer to find information about other café bookstores in the area.

Unit A

Internet

Understanding Web Browsers

A **computer network** consists of two or more computers that can share information and resources. An **intranet** is a computer network that connects computers in a local area only, such as computers in a company's office. The **Internet** is a communications system that connects computers and computer networks located around the world. An estimated 40 million computers are currently connected to the Internet through telephone lines, cables, satellites, and other telecommunications media, as shown in Figure A-1. Through the Internet, these computers can share many types of information, including text, graphics, sounds, videos, and computer programs. Anyone who has access to a computer and a connection to the Internet through a computer network or modem can use this rich information source. The **World Wide Web** (the **Web** or **WWW**) is a part of the Internet containing Web pages that are linked together. Web pages contain highlighted words, phrases, or graphics called **hyperlinks**, or simply **links**, that open other Web pages when you click them. Figure A-2 shows a sample Web page. A page's links can also open graphics files or play sound or video files. **Web browsers** are software programs used to access and display Web pages. Web browsers, such as Microsoft Internet Explorer and Netscape Navigator, make navigating the Web easy by providing a graphical, point-and-click environment. This unit features **Internet Explorer 5**, a popular browser from Microsoft that comes with Microsoft Office 2000. Although you only use the Internet Explorer Web browser in this unit, the Internet Explorer 5 suite contains other network communications options that are listed in Table A-1. Alice uses Internet Explorer and the Web to find information about bookstore cafés in southern Florida that might be potential MediaLoft competitors.

Details

Using Internet Explorer, Alice can:

Display Web pages
Alice can access Web pages from all over the world for many business purposes. For example, she can check the pages of competing book retailers to see how they market their products.

Use links to move from one Web page to another
Alice can use the hyperlinks on competing book retailers' Web pages to get more specific information about their operations.

Play audio and video clips
A Web browser can play audio and video clips if it has been configured to do so and your computer has the appropriate hardware, such as speakers. Alice might find some book retailers' Web sites that include links to short video clips of store interiors or sound clips from audio products that they sell.

Search the Web for information
Alice can utilize various search programs in her Web browser to look for more information on bookstore-related topics such as discounts and shipping policies.

Save a list of favorite Web pages
Alice can use Internet Explorer to save a list of Web pages that she might need to visit again, such as a page for a competing bookstore. By adding a Web page to her list of favorites, it is easy for her to return to the page later.

Print or save the text and graphics on Web pages
If Alice finds information or images that she wants to keep a hard copy of, she can easily print the entire Web page, including any graphics. She can also save the text or graphics on a Web page, or copy this information temporarily to the Clipboard, where it is available for pasting into other Windows programs.

FIGURE A-1: Internet structure

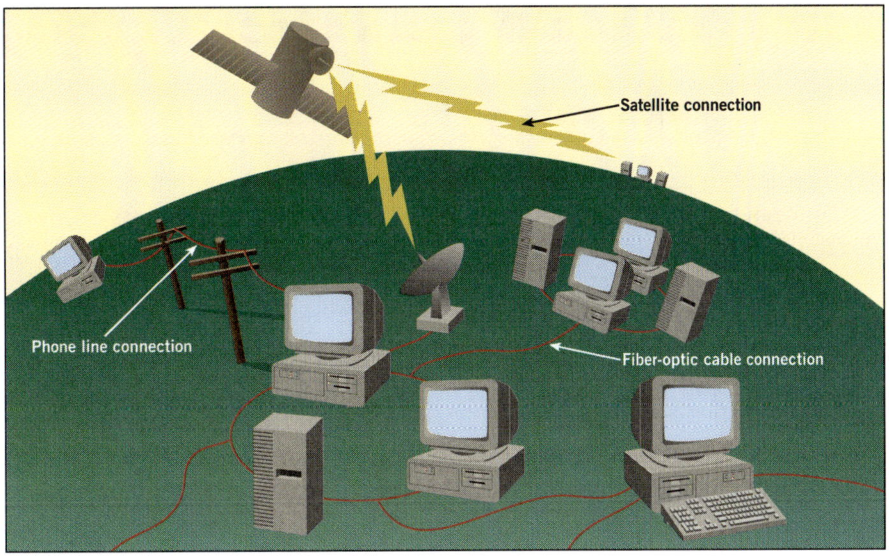

FIGURE A-2: Sample Web page

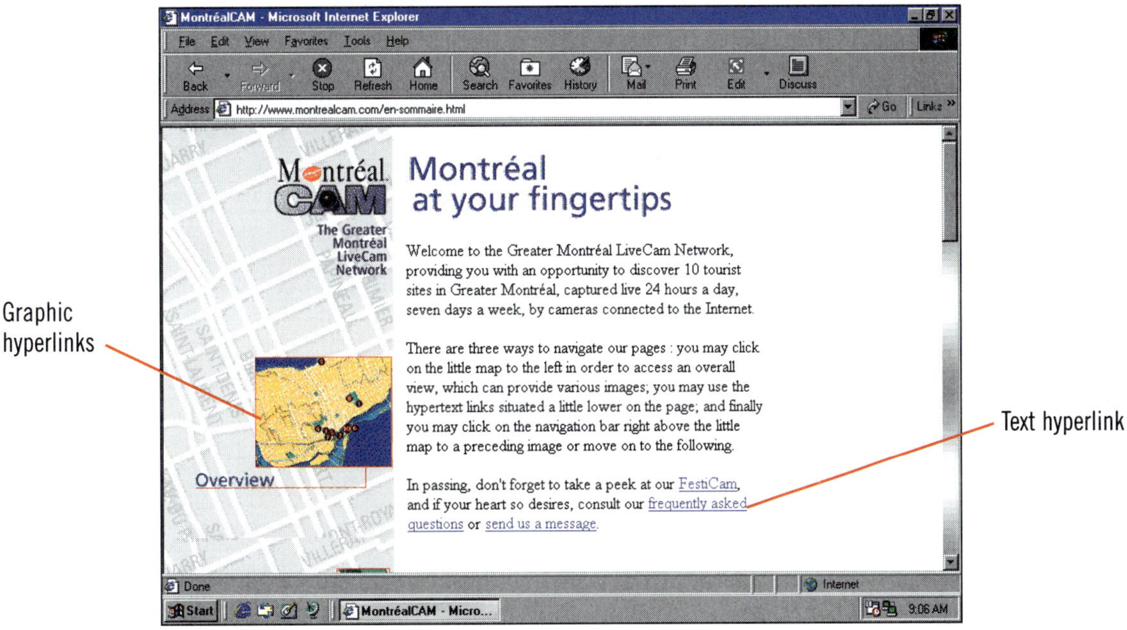

TABLE A-1: Internet Explorer 5 suite components

feature	description
FrontPage Express	Provides tools for creating new Web pages and editing existing ones
Internet Explorer	Lets you view and print Web pages
NetMeeting	Enables you to set up audio and video links to people at different locations for a live discussion
Outlook Express	Allows you to read and send e-mail messages as well as read and post messages in newsgroups (discussions organized around specific topics)
Personal Web Server	Lets you use your personal computer to host a Web site
Web Publishing Wizard	Lets you publish your Web page files, support files, and other Web content files on a Web server
Windows Media Player	Lets you listen to and/or view live and prerecorded sounds, images, and videos

Unit A

Internet

Starting Internet Explorer

Internet Explorer is a Web browser that connects your computer to the Web using an Internet connection. After Internet Explorer 5 is installed, its icon appears on your Windows desktop. You can also start Internet Explorer by clicking the Internet Explorer icon on the Quick Launch toolbar. The exact location of the Internet Explorer icon might vary on different computers. See your instructor or technical support person for assistance if you are unable to locate the Internet Explorer icon or if you do not have an Internet connection. Before Alice can take advantage of the Web's many features to find more information about competing bookstores, she must start Internet Explorer.

Steps

1. If you connect to the Internet using a modem and a telephone, follow your normal procedure to establish your connection
2. Locate the **Internet Explorer icon** on your Windows desktop
   The icon should appear on the left side of your screen, as shown in Figure A-3. If the icon is not on your desktop, click the Start button on the taskbar, point to Programs on the Start menu, and then click Internet Explorer. Skip Step 3.
3. Double-click the **Internet Explorer icon** on the Windows desktop
   Internet Explorer opens and displays your home page, which might look different from the one shown in Figure A-4. A **home page** is the first page that opens every time you start Internet Explorer. Your home page might be one for your school, employer, or one that you specify.
4. If necessary, click the **Maximize button** on the Internet Explorer title bar to maximize the program window

Trouble?

If a Dial-up Connection or an Internet Connection Wizard dialog box opens, you will need to either connect to the Internet or enter your Internet settings to complete the step. See your instructor or technical support person for assistance.

CLUES TO USE

History of the Internet and the World Wide Web

The Internet has its roots in the United States Department of Defense Advanced Research Projects Agency Network (ARPANET), which began in 1969. In 1986, the National Science Foundation formed NSFNET, which replaced ARPANET. NSFNET expanded the foundation of the U.S. portion of the Internet with high-speed, long-distance lines. In 1991, the U.S. Congress further expanded the Internet's capacity and speed and opened it to commercial use. Over 200 countries now have Internet access.

The World Wide Web was created in Switzerland in 1991 to allow links between documents on the Internet. Software programs designed to access the Web (called Web browsers) use common "point-and-click" interfaces. The first graphical Web browser, Mosaic, was introduced at the University of Illinois in 1993. Microsoft Internet Explorer and Netscape Navigator are two current, popular Web browsers.

FIGURE A-3: Internet Explorer icon on desktop

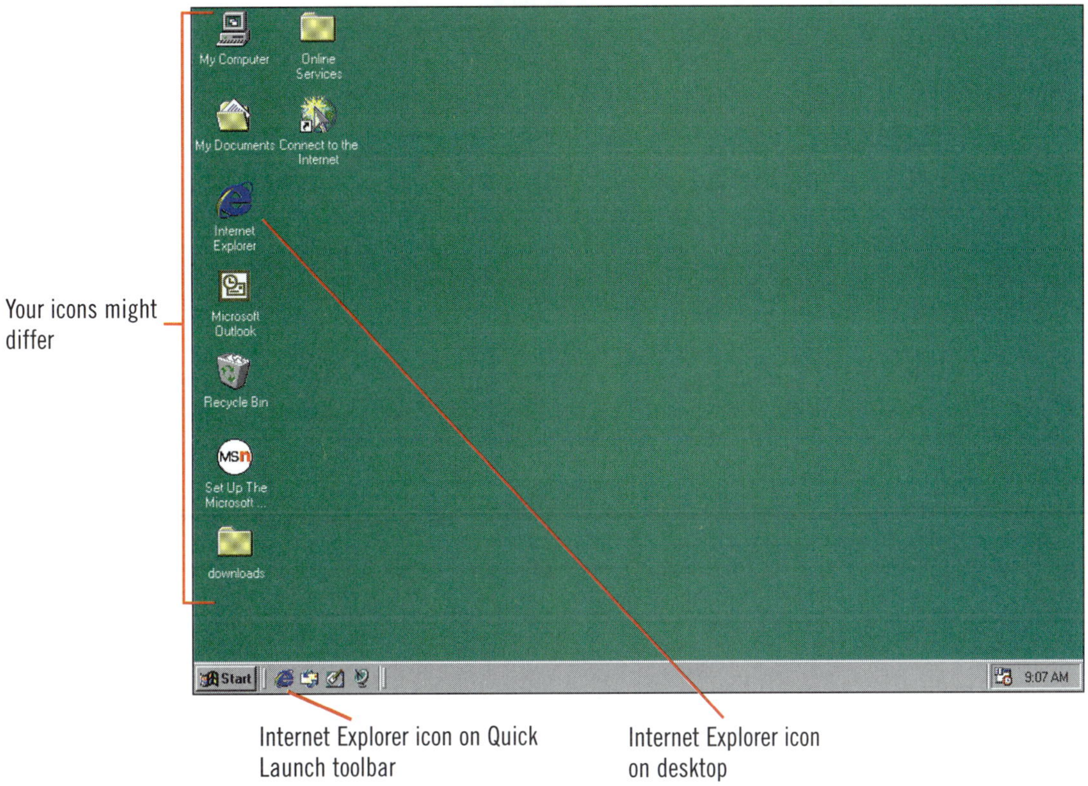

FIGURE A-4: Sample Web page for Microsoft Corporation

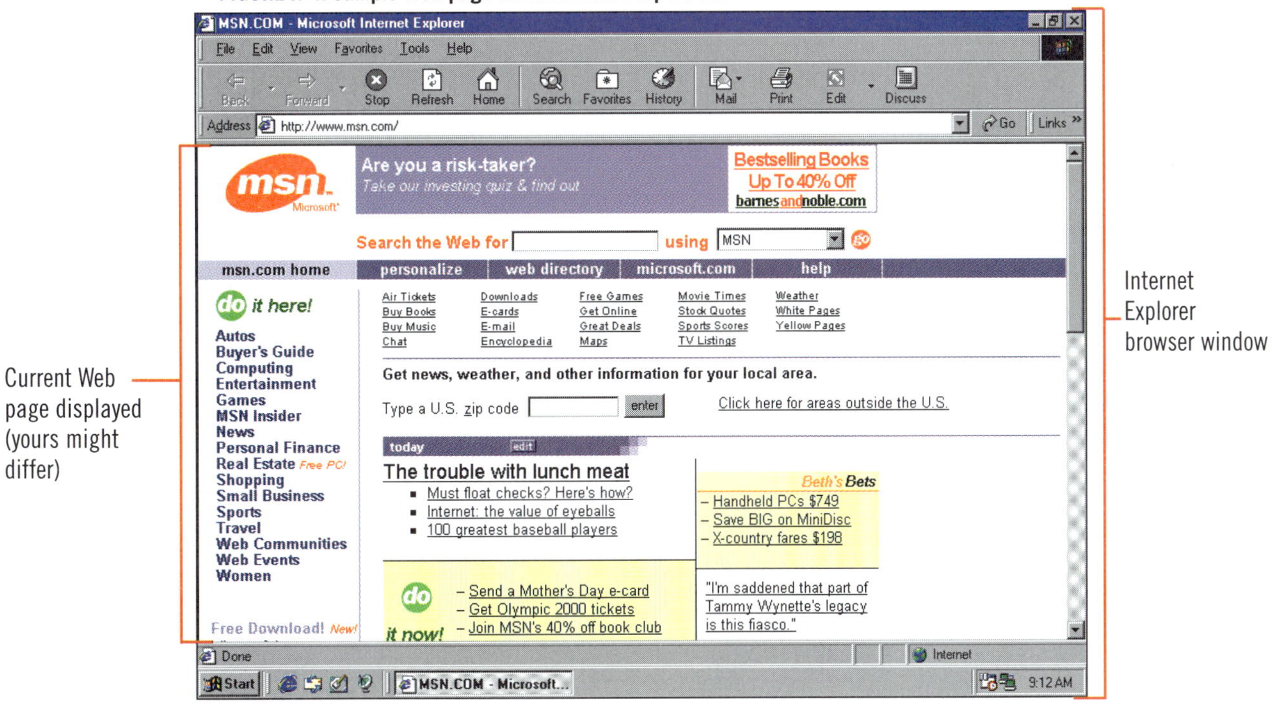

Internet

Unit A

Internet

Exploring the Browser Window

The elements of the Internet Explorer browser window shown in Figure A-5 let you view, print, and search for information on the Web. You can customize the toolbar and Address bar, so your screen might look different than the one shown in Figure A-5. Before using, or **surfing**, the Web, Alice needs to become more familiar with the components of the Internet Explorer browser window. Find and compare the elements below, using Figure A-5 as a guide.

Details

- The **title bar** at the top of the page usually contains the name of the Web page currently displayed in the Web browser window.
- The **menu bar** provides access to most of the browser's features through a variety of commands, similar to other Office programs.
- The **toolbar** provides buttons for many options, such as stopping the transfer of a Web page, moving from one Web page to another, printing Web pages, and searching for information on the Internet. Table A-2 explains these buttons. Many commonly used commands available on menus are more readily accessed using the toolbar buttons.
- The **Address bar** displays the address of the Web page currently opened. The **Uniform Resource Locator** (**URL**), or the Web page's address, appears in the Address bar after you open (or load) the page.
- The **status indicator** (the Internet Explorer logo) animates while a new Web page loads.
- The **Web page area** (or **document window**) is the specific area where the current Web page appears. You might need to scroll down the page to view its entire contents.
- The **vertical scroll bar** allows you to move the current Web page up or down in the browser window. The **scroll box** indicates your relative position within the Web page.
- The **status bar** performs three main functions: 1) displays information about your connection progress whenever you open a new Web page; 2) notifies you when you connect to another Web site; and 3) identifies the percentage of information transferred from the Web server to your browser. The status bar also displays the Web addresses of any links on the Web page when you move your mouse pointer over them.

FIGURE A-5: Elements of the Internet Explorer window

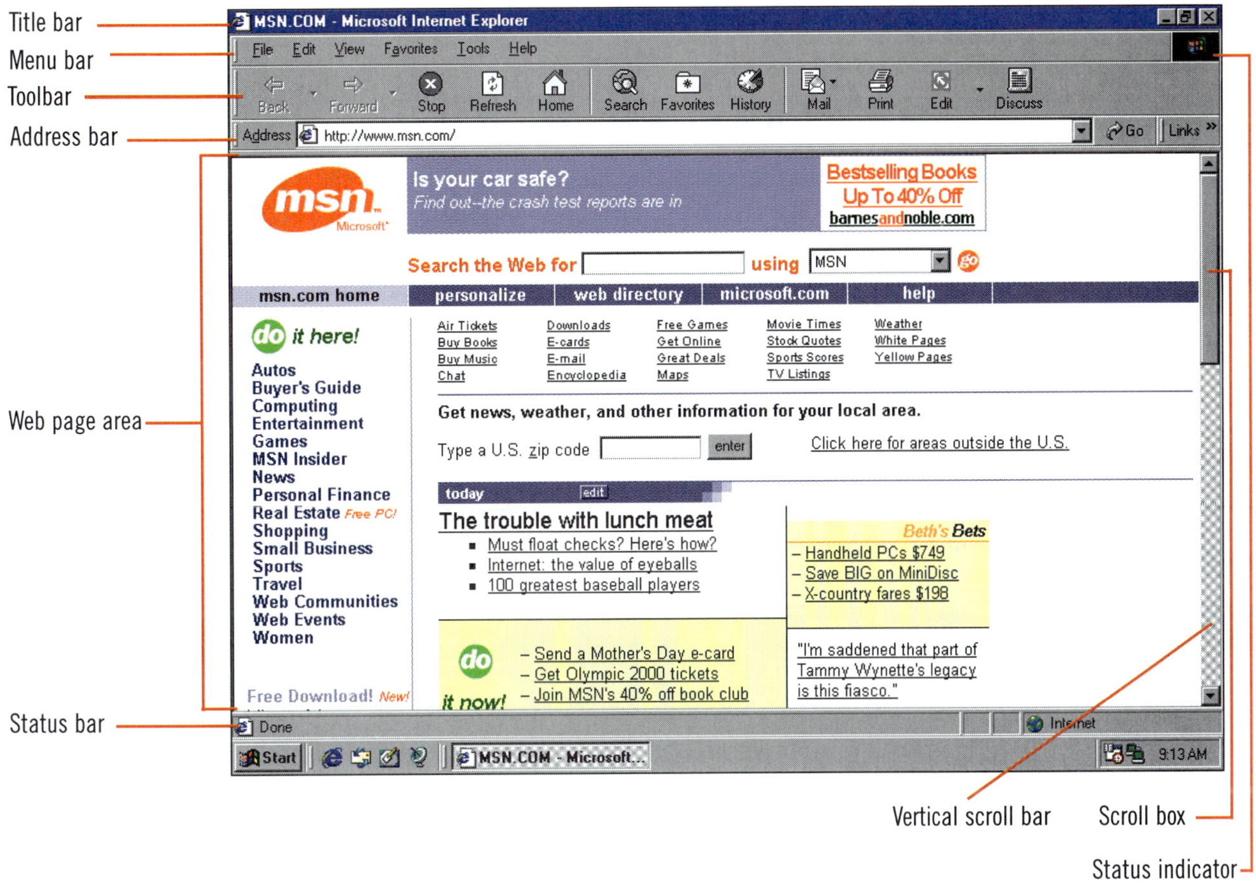

TABLE A-2: Toolbar buttons

button name	button	description
Back		Opens the previous page
Forward		Opens the next page
Stop		Stops loading the page
Refresh		Refreshes the contents of the current page
Home		Opens the home page
Search		Opens the Search Assistant in the Explorer Search bar
Favorites		Opens the Explorer Favorites bar
History		Opens the Explorer History bar
Mail		Displays options for working with mail and news
Print		Prints the current Web page
Edit		Transfers the currently displayed Web page to Microsoft FrontPage for editing
Discuss		Lets you add or edit discussion servers and opens the Discussion bar

Unit A

Internet

Opening and Saving a URL

As you learned in the previous lesson, the address for a Web page is also called a URL. Each Web page has a unique URL beginning with "http" (which stands for Hypertext Transfer Protocol) followed by a colon, two forward slashes, and the Web site's name. After the name of the Web site, another slash and one or more folder names and a filename might appear. For example, in the address http://www.course.com/Illustrated/MediaLoft/commune.html, the name of the Web site is *www.course.com*; a folder at that site is *Illustrated*; and within the Illustrated/MediaLoft folder is a file named *commune.html*. The Internet Explorer **Favorites list** allows you to create your own list of frequently visited Web pages that you can then access without having to type a URL. After you add a Web page to your Favorites list, you can automatically access that page by clicking the Favorites button on the toolbar and then clicking its name, or by clicking the favorite's name on the Favorites menu. Alice wants to investigate the Web page for a local competitor, Miami Booksellers. Since she will return to this site often as she completes her research, she adds it to her Favorites list.

Steps

1. **Click anywhere in the Address bar**
   The current address is highlighted; any text you type replaces it.

2. **Type www.course.com/Illustrated/MediaLoft/MiamiBooksellers/index.html**
   Internet Explorer will automatically add the http:// protocol to the beginning of the address you type after you press [Enter].

3. **Press [Enter]**
   The status bar displays the connection process. After a few seconds, the Web page for Miami Booksellers opens in the Web page area, as shown in Figure A-6.

4. **Click Favorites on the menu bar, click Add to Favorites; if necessary, in the Name text box of the Add Favorite dialog box type Miami Booksellers, then click OK**
   The name and URL for Miami Booksellers are added to your Favorites list.

5. **Click the Back button on the toolbar**
   The previous Web page appears in the Web page area.

QuickTip

You can change the favorite's default page name by typing a new name in the Name text box.

CLUES TO USE

Creating and organizing favorites

Once you add a Web page to your Favorites list, returning to that page is much easier. To keep your Favorites list manageable, you only should add pages that you expect to visit again. To add a Web page to your Favorites list, open the Web page in the browser window, click Favorites on the menu bar, click Add to Favorites, then click OK.

If your Favorites list gets too long, you can organize the page names into folders. To add a folder to your Favorites list, click Favorites on the menu bar, click Organize Favorites, and then click the Create Folder button. You can use the buttons or drag and drop to move the favorites into different folders.

FIGURE A-6: Web page for Miami Booksellers

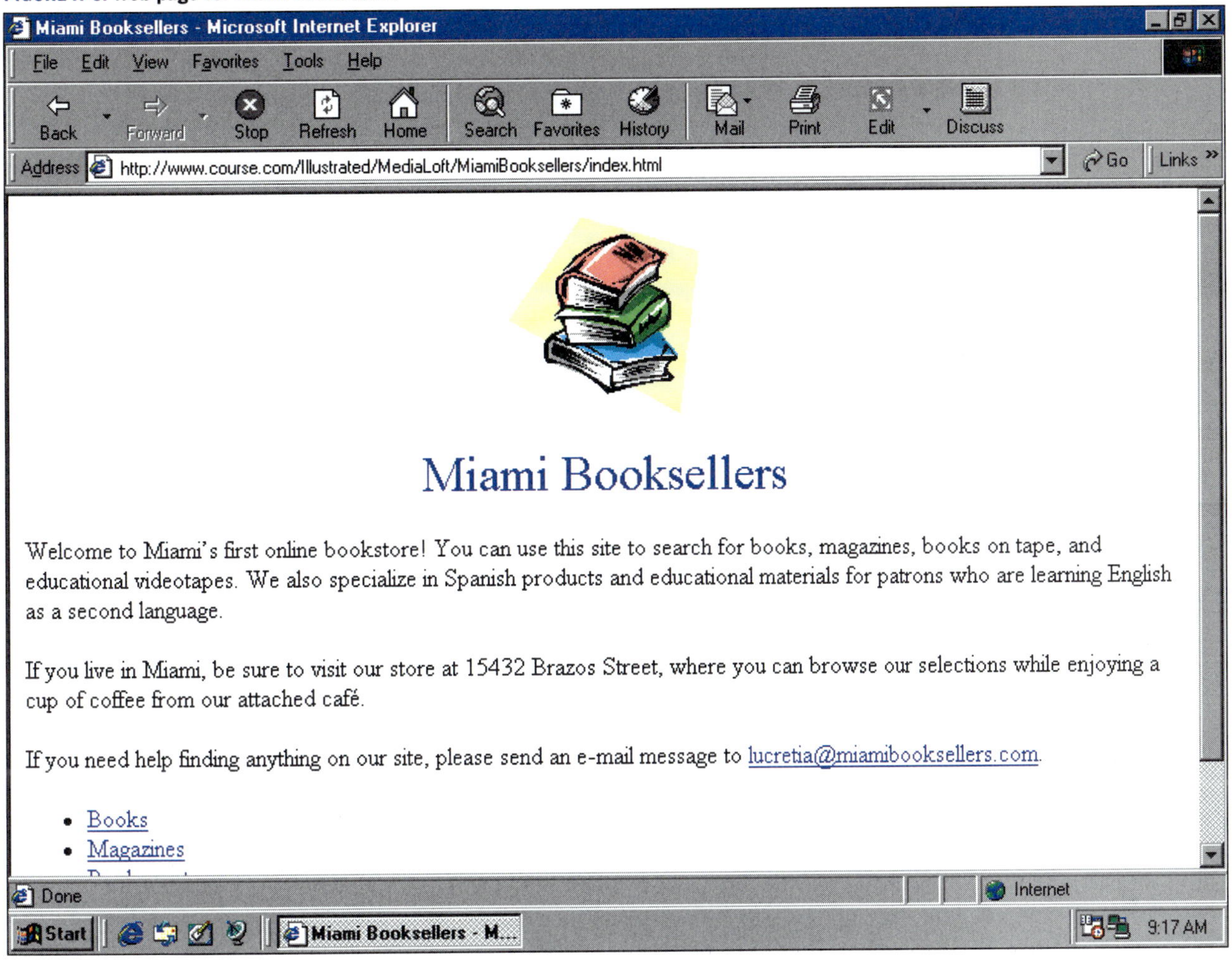

Internet

Unit A

Internet

Navigating Web Pages

Hyperlinks enable you to navigate to, or open, another location on the same Web page or jump to an entirely different Web page. You can follow these links to obtain more information about a topic by clicking the highlighted word or phrase. If you change your mind or if a page takes too long to load, you can click the Stop button on the toolbar. While viewing the Web page for Miami Booksellers, Alice decides to investigate the Books link to see what types of books Miami Booksellers features.

Steps

1. Click **Favorites** on the menu bar
2. Click **Miami Booksellers**
   The Web page for Miami Booksellers that you added to your Favorites list opens in the Web page area.
3. If necessary, click the **vertical scroll bar** to move down the Web page until you see the link **Books**, then place your mouse pointer on the link
   As shown in Figure A-7, the mouse pointer changes to when you place it over an active link.
4. Click **Books**
   The status indicator animates as the new Web page loads. The Books Web page opens in your Web browser window, as shown in Figure A-8.
5. Click the **Home button** on the toolbar
   The initial Web page that opens when you start Internet Explorer reappears in your Web browser window.

Trouble?

If you receive an error message, click a different link on the page. If you want to cancel loading the page, click the Stop button on the toolbar.

Clues to Use

Selecting a home page

When you click , the page that is specified as "home" opens in your Web browser window. When you install Internet Explorer, the default home page is a page at the Microsoft Web site. You can easily select a different home page to open each time you start Internet Explorer or when you click . Simply open that page in your Web browser window, click Tools on the menu bar, click Internet Options, click the General tab, click Use Current, then click OK to specify the current page as your home page.

FIGURE A-7: Hyperlinks on Miami Booksellers Web page

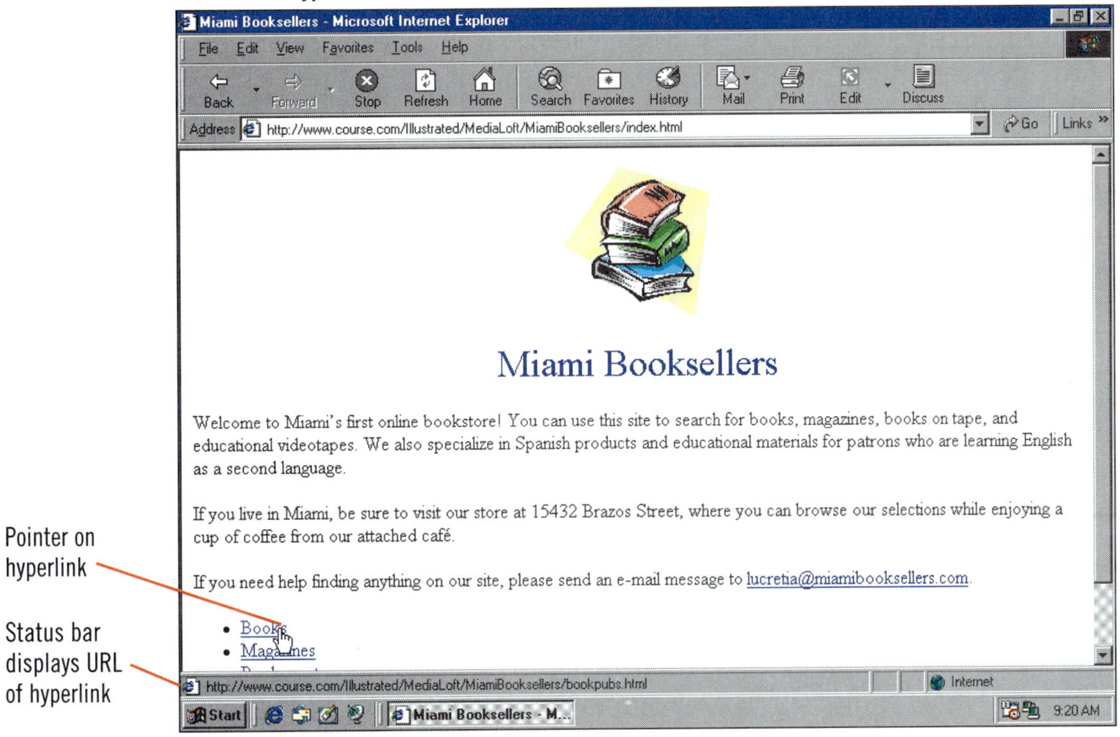

FIGURE A-8: Books Web page

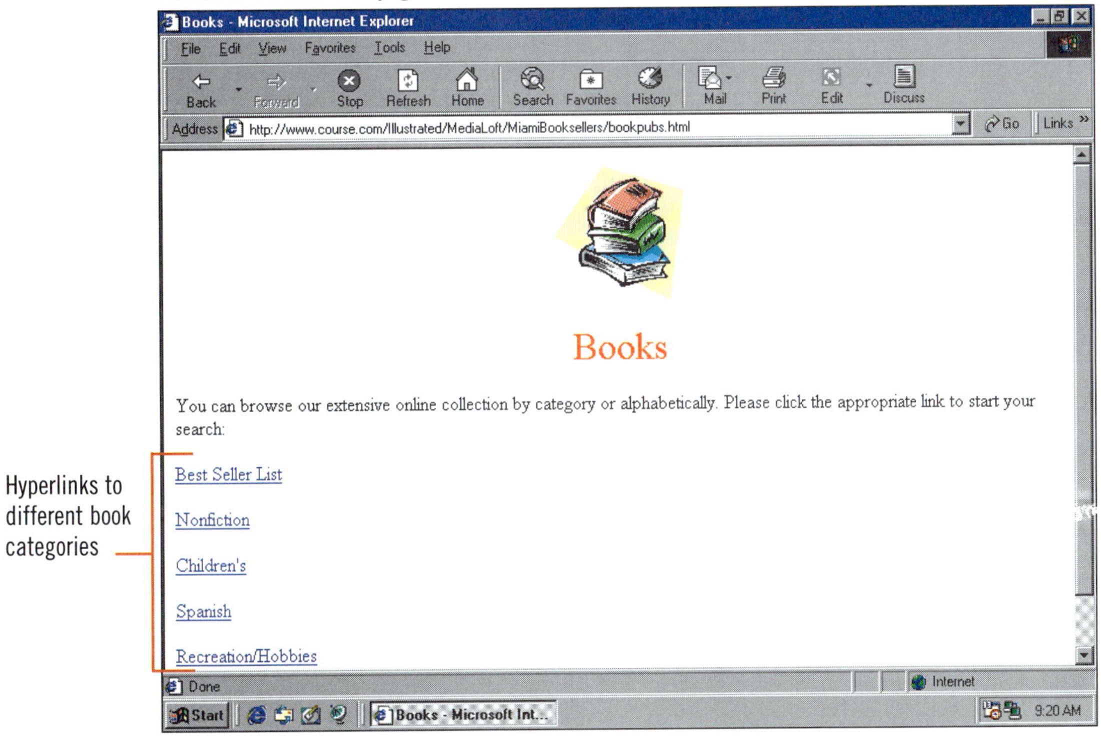

Internet

Unit A

Internet

Getting Help

Internet Explorer provides a Help system with information and instructions on various features and commands. While exploring the Web pages for bookstores, Alice discovers one with very small type. She decides to access the Help system to find instructions for increasing the type's font size.

Steps

1. Click **Help** on the menu bar
   The Help menu opens.
2. Click **Contents and Index**
   The Microsoft Internet Explorer Help dialog box opens, as shown in Figure A-9, with the Contents tab selected. Table A-3 explains how each of the three tabs provides a different way to access Help information.
3. Click the **Search tab**
   The Search tab allows you to search for a specific word or phrase.
4. In the Type in the keyword to find text box, type **font sizes**, then click **List Topics**
   As shown in Figure A-10, a list of relevant topics appears in the Select Topic to display list box.
5. In the Select Topic to display list box, double-click **Display text larger or smaller**
   As shown in Figure A-11, the text in the right pane of the Microsoft Internet Explorer Help window provides information on how to change the font size.
6. Click the **Close button** in the upper-right corner of the Microsoft Internet Explorer Help window
   The Help window closes.

Trouble?

Don't worry if a different tab is selected. Continue with Step 3.

QuickTip

You can also press [Enter] instead of clicking List Topics to display the relevant topics.

TABLE A-3: Help options

tab	function
Contents	Lists the categories available in Help
Index	Lists available Help topics in alphabetical order, and lets you locate specific topics
Search	Locates the desired Help topic based on the keyword or phrase you enter

FIGURE A-9: Microsoft Internet Explorer Help window

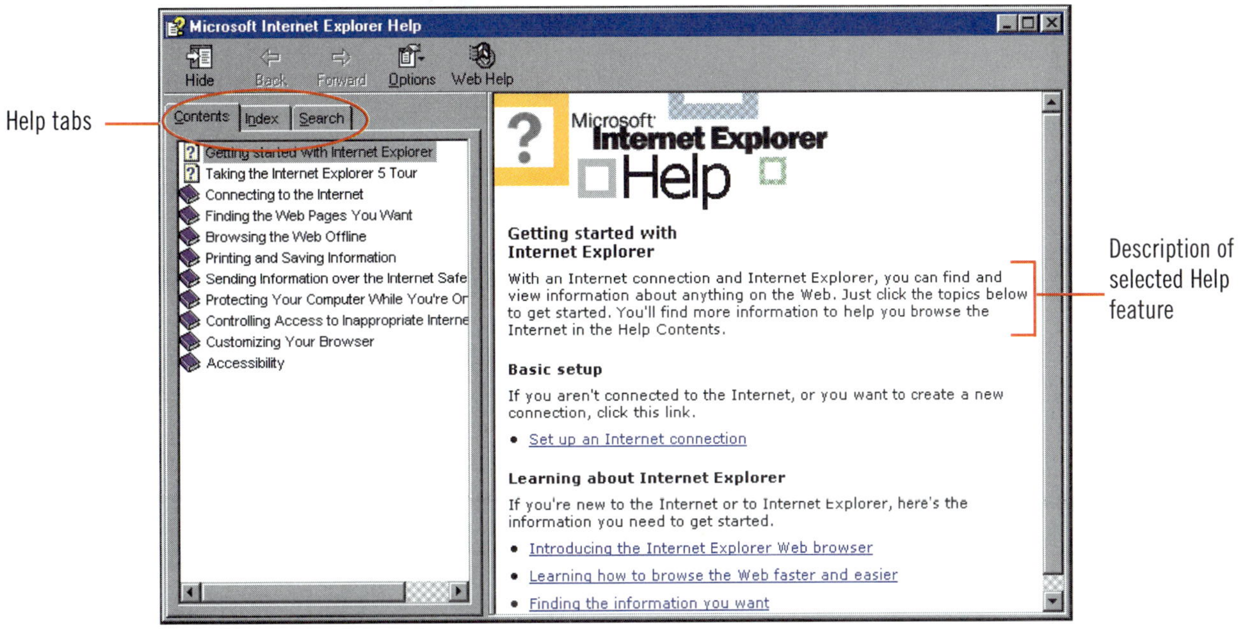

FIGURE A-10: Search tab

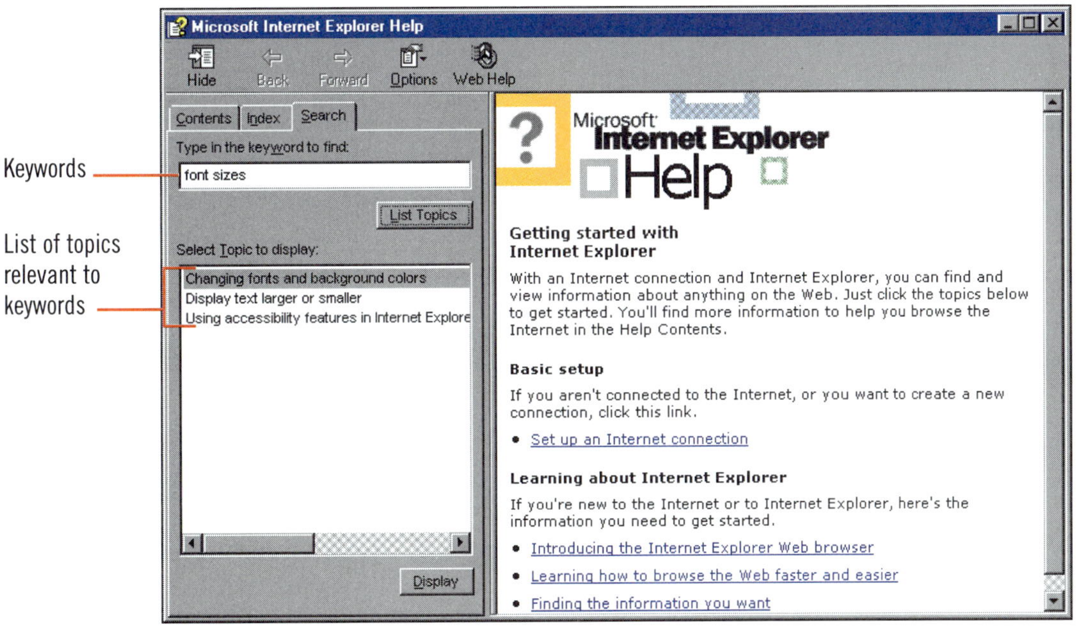

FIGURE A-11: Help information

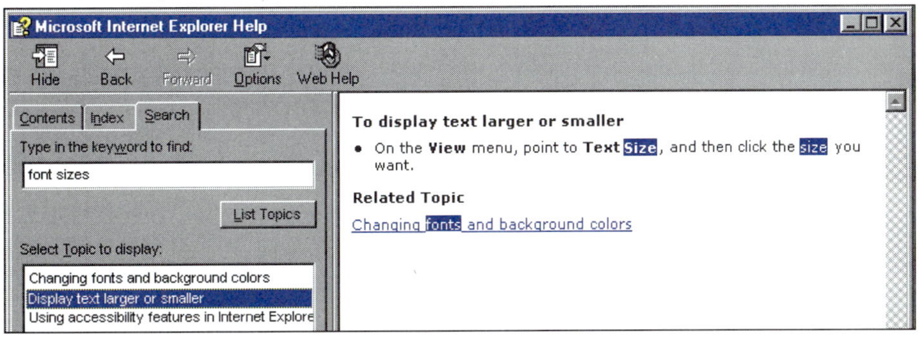

Internet

Printing a Web Page

You can quickly print the Web page that currently appears in the Web page area by clicking the Print button on the toolbar. When you click File on the menu bar, and then click Print, the options in the Print dialog box allow you to specify parameters such as the number of copies and the page ranges you want to print. When you print a Web page, its text and any graphics will appear on your hard copy. Table A-4 explains printing options in more detail. Alice decides to print two copies of the Miami Booksellers Web page: one for her files and the other to attach to a summary memo that outlines her research results.

Steps

1. Click the **Back button** on the toolbar to return to the Miami Booksellers home page

QuickTip

To print a Web page without changing any settings, click on the toolbar.

2. Click **File** on the menu bar, then click **Print**
   The Print dialog box opens, as shown in Figure A-12.

3. In the Copies area, click the **Number of copies up arrow** until the number **2** appears
   The selection of 2 indicates that two copies will be printed.

4. Make sure your computer is connected to a printer that is turned on and contains paper

Trouble?

If your computer is not connected to a printer or if an error message appears, see your instructor or technical support person for assistance.

5. Click **OK**
   The Print dialog box closes, and two copies of the current Web page print.

CLUES TO USE

Copying information from a Web page

As with other Office programs, you can select text or information on a Web page and use the Copy and Paste commands to use the same information in another program, such as Word. You can also save a graphic image from a Web page by right-clicking the image, clicking Save Picture As on the pop-up menu, and then specifying where to save the image. If you just need to copy an image, click the Copy command on the pop-up menu. Using the Copy command saves the text or image to the Clipboard.

Keep in mind that the same laws that protect printed works generally protect information and graphics published on a Web page. Do not use material on a Web page without citing its source and checking the site carefully for any usage restrictions.

FIGURE A-12: Print dialog box

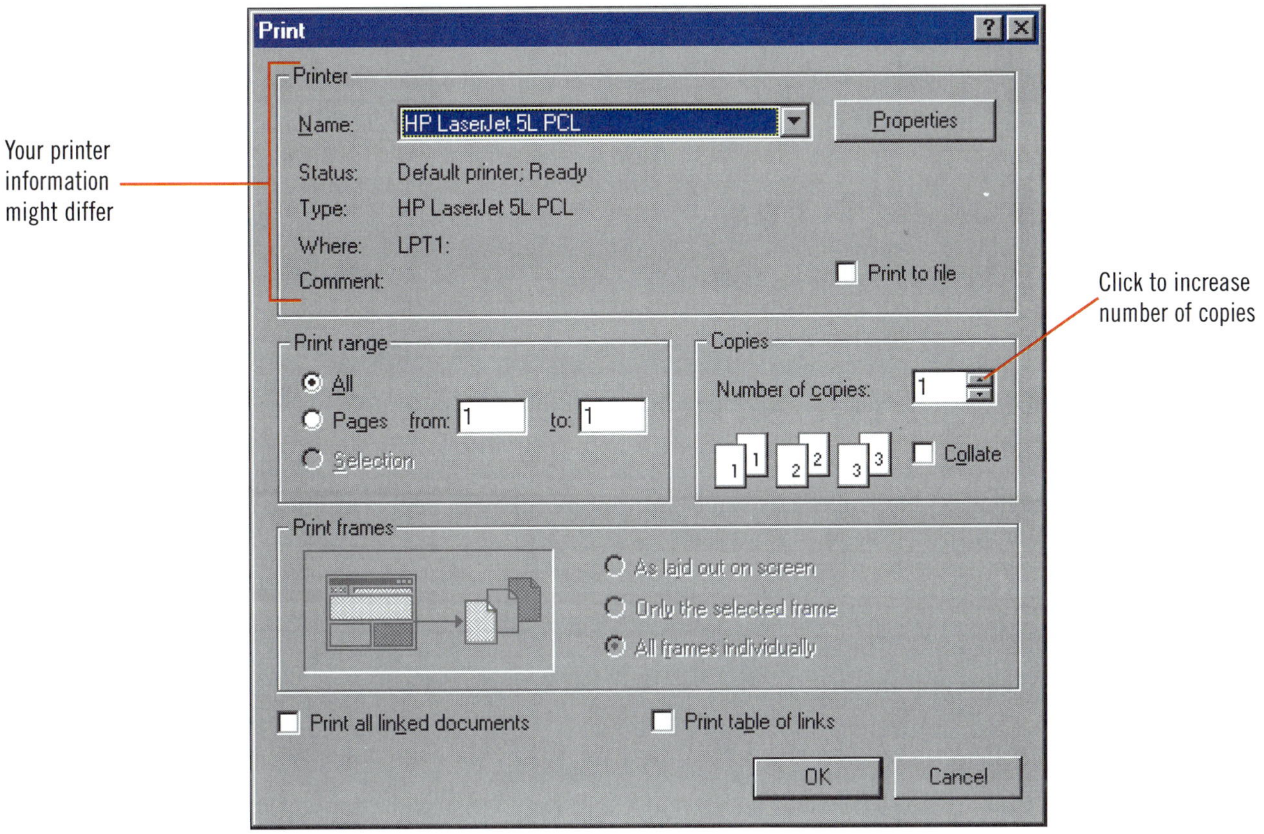

TABLE A-4: Printing options

option	description
Printer	Displays information about the name, status, type, and location of the active printer
Properties	Allows you to specify parameters such as paper size, paper source, and orientation
Print range	Allows you to choose to print all pages, a range of pages, or a selection on a page
Copies	Indicates the number of copies of each page to print and their sequence
Print frames	Allows you to print only the current frame or all frames separately or together
Print all linked documents	Opens and prints each document referenced by a link on the current page
Print table of links	Prints links in a table at the end of the document

Unit A

Internet

Searching for Information on the Internet

An estimated 100 to 600 million Web pages and other information sources are available through the Internet. At times, finding the information you want seems like looking for the proverbial needle in the haystack. Luckily, you can use Web **search engines** to help you locate useful information. You simply enter a keyword or phrase describing the information you want to find, and the search engine provides you with a list of related Web sites. Each of these Web sites are listed as hyperlinks so you can quickly and easily continue your search. Alice's final task is to find information about competing bookstores that will help her to recommend a decision about MediaLoft's potential expansion into southern Florida. She decides to use Internet Explorer's built-in shortcuts to conduct her search.

Steps

1. **Click the Search button on the toolbar**

   As shown in Figure A-13, the Web page area splits into two panes. The **Explorer Search bar** opens in the left pane and contains the **Search Assistant**, which displays a list of search options for finding Web pages, people, businesses, previous searches, or maps. The right pane shows the Web page you were viewing before beginning your search.

2. **In the Explorer Search bar, make sure the Find a Web page option button is selected, click the Find a Web page containing text box, then type bookstore cafes**

   Now that you've specified your search keywords, you can initiate the search.

3. **Click Search**

   Your search results appear as a list of related Web sites, called **hits**. See Figure A-14. Some search engines list hits by category or topic, whereas others list Web page names. You can click any hyperlink to open the Web page or a list of Web pages for a category.

4. **Examine the hit list by scrolling it up or down in the Explorer Search bar, then click a hyperlink of your choice**

   The related page containing more information about bookstore cafés opens in the right pane. When you finish exploring the hyperlinked site, you can continue or end your search.

5. **Click the Home button, then click**

   Your home page appears in the right pane, and then the Explorer Search bar closes.

CLUES TO USE

Search engines

Many search engines, such as Yahoo, Infoseek, Lycos, WebCrawler, and Excite, can help you locate information on the Internet. These search engines routinely use software programs to methodically catalog, or **crawl**, through the entire Internet and create huge databases with links to Web pages and their URLs. When you enter a keyword or phrase, the search engine examines its database index for relevant information and displays a list of Web sites.

Each search engine differs slightly in the way it formats information, records the number of Internet sites in the database, and how often it updates the database. If you don't find what you need using one search engine, try running the same search using a different search engine or search phrase until you find what you need. Most people develop personal favorites and learn which engine works best in various situations.

FIGURE A-13: Search Assistant in the Explorer Search bar

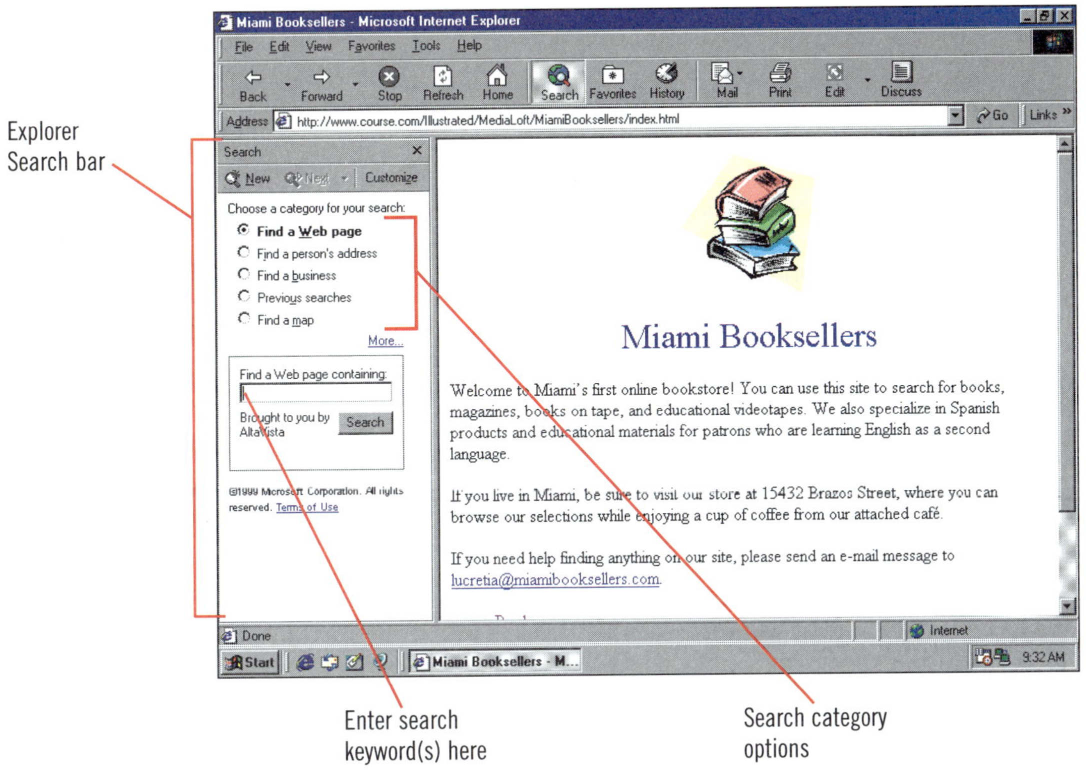

FIGURE A-14: Bookstore-related Web sites

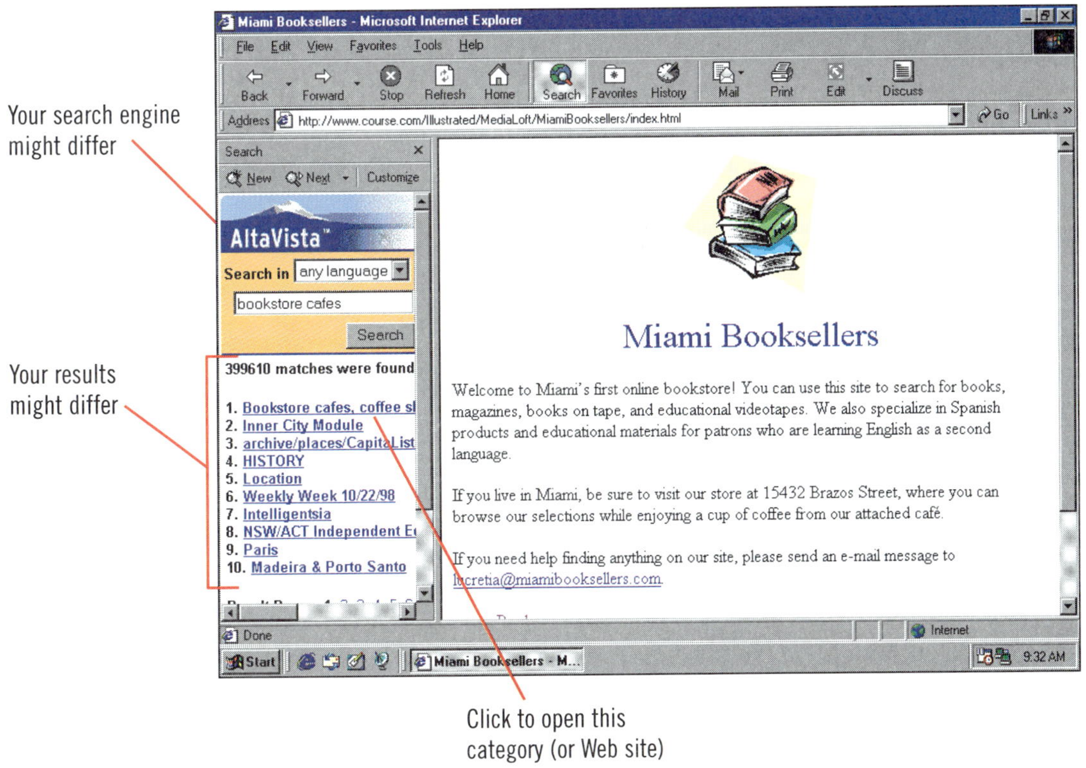

Internet

Unit A

Internet

Exiting Internet Explorer

When you are ready to exit Internet Explorer, you can click the Close button in the upper-right corner of the browser window or select the Close command on the File menu. You do not need to save files before you exit because all files you view with Internet Explorer are already saved on your computer or on another computer connected to the network you are using. Alice completes her bookstore research on the Web and is ready to exit Internet Explorer.

Steps

1. Click **File** on the menu bar
   The File menu opens, as shown in Figure A-15.
2. Click **Close** on the File menu
   The Internet Explorer browser window closes.
3. If you connected to the Internet by telephone, follow your normal procedure to close your connection

QuickTip

You can also exit from Internet Explorer by clicking the Close button in the upper-right corner of the browser window.

Clues to Use

Saving or sending a Web page

Before exiting from Internet Explorer, you may want to save a copy of the current page or send someone a copy. By selecting Save As on the File menu, you can choose to save the complete Web page, including any graphics—or just the text from the page—in a file on your computer. If you want to send the complete page to someone, point to Send on the File menu, click Page By E-mail, and then use your e-mail program to address and send the message to the intended recipient.

FIGURE A-15: Internet Explorer with File menu open

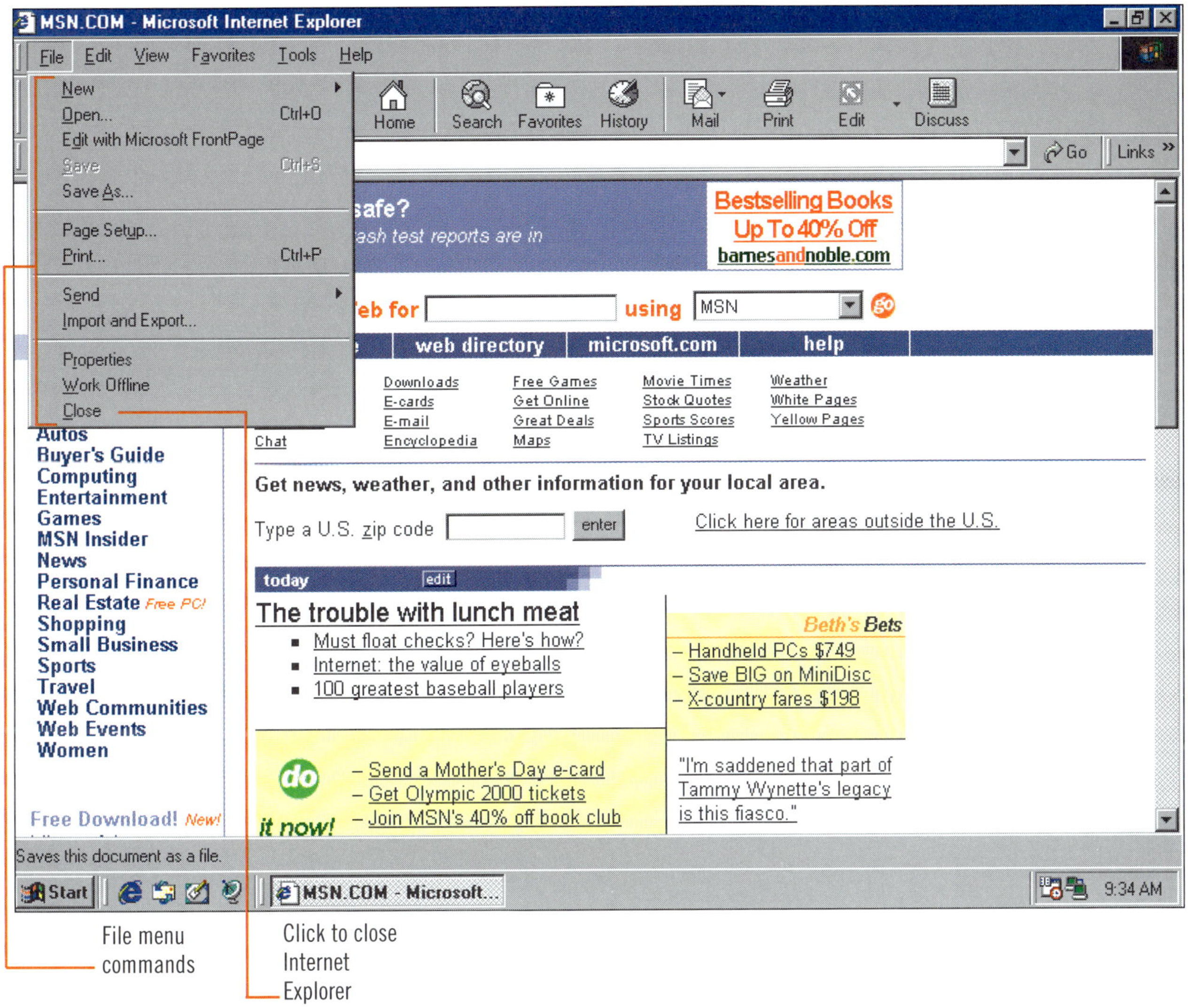

Internet

Practice

▶ Concepts Review

Label each element of the Internet Explorer browser window shown in Figure A-16.

FIGURE A-16

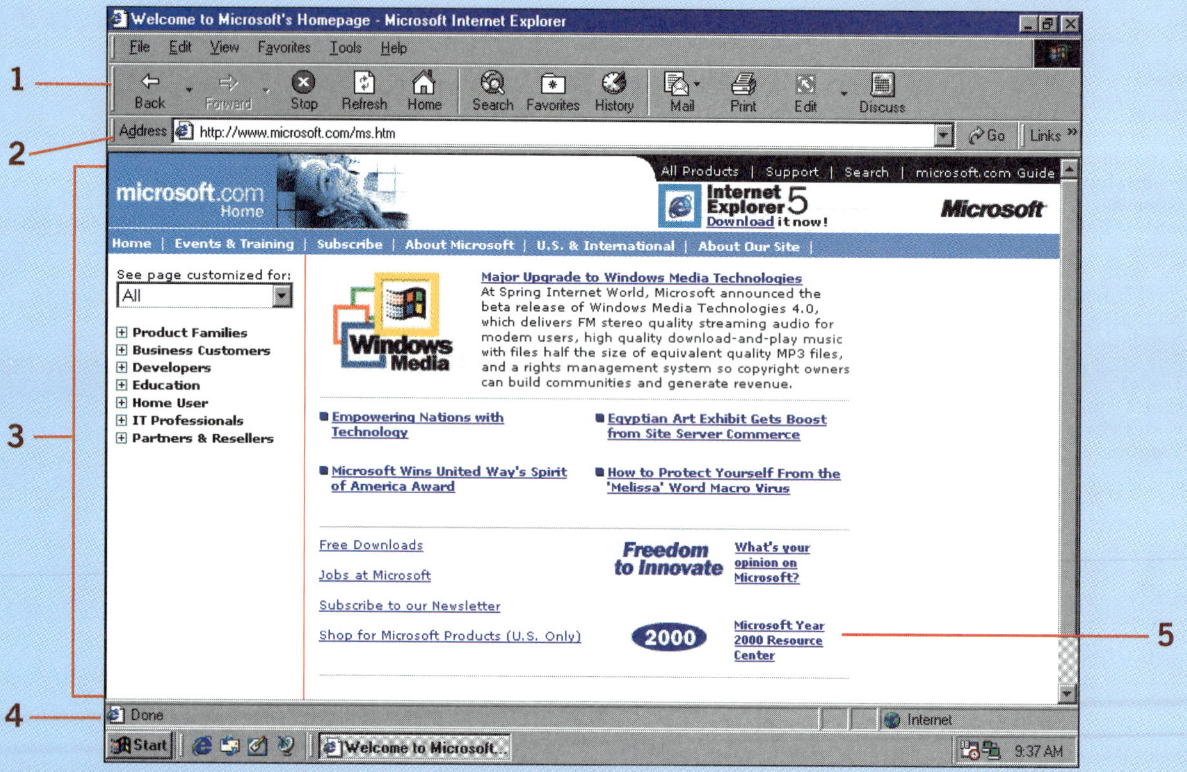

Match each term with the statement that describes it.

6. Address bar	**a.** Animates when Internet Explorer loads a page
7. Toolbar	**b.** Displays the URL for the currently displayed page
8. Favorites button	**c.** Provides shortcuts for options on the menu bar
9. Status indicator	**d.** Displays a list of selected Web pages
10. Back button	**e.** Displays the previously viewed page

Select the best answer from the list of choices.

11. Software programs used to access and display Web pages are called
- a. Web sites.
- b. Web windows.
- c. Web documents.
- d. Web browsers.

12. If you want to save the name and URL of a file and return to it later, you can add it to a list called
- a. Favorites.
- b. Bookmarks.
- c. Home pages.
- d. Preferences.

13. An international telecommunications network that consists of hyperlinked documents is called
- a. NSFNET.
- b. Netscape Navigator.
- c. Internet Explorer.
- d. the World Wide Web.

14. Where are the buttons that perform many common functions, such as printing, located in Internet Explorer?
- a. Address bar
- b. Toolbar
- c. Status bar
- d. Menu bar

15. Most Web pages are longer than the browser window. Which feature must you use to view the entire page?
- a. Scroll bar
- b. Status bar
- c. Forward button
- d. Home button

16. Which of the following URLs is valid?
- a. http://www.usf.edu
- b. htp://www.usf.edu
- c. http:/www.usf.edu
- d. http//www.usf.edu

17. Which button should you click if you want to stop a Web page that is currently loading on your computer?
- a. 
- b. 
- c. 
- d. 

18. Highlighted or underlined words that allow you to navigate to another Web page location are called
- a. Explorers.
- b. Favorites.
- c. Web browsers.
- d. Hyperlinks.

19. The URL of the Web page currently displayed in your Web browser window appears in the
- a. Title bar.
- b. Browser window.
- c. Address bar.
- d. Status bar.

20. To locate information on a specific topic on the Internet, you can use a
- a. URL locator.
- b. Web browser.
- c. Favorites list.
- d. Search engine.

Skills Review

1. **Start Internet Explorer.**
   a. Make sure your computer is connected to the Internet.
   b. Start Internet Explorer.

2. **Explore the browser window.**
   a. Identify the toolbar, menu bar, Address bar, status bar, status indicator, URL, browser window, and scroll bars.
   b. Identify the toolbar buttons for printing, searching, viewing favorites, and returning to the home page.
   c. Identify the complete URL of the current Web page.

3. **Open and save a URL.**
   a. Open the Web page www.cnet.com using the Address bar.
   b. Explore the site by using the scroll bars, toolbar, and hyperlinks.
   c. Open the Web page www.loc.gov using the Address bar.
   d. Add the current Web page to your Favorites list.
   e. Click the Home button.
   f. Click the Favorites button.
   g. Click Library of Congress Home Page to return to that page.
   h. Close the Explorer Favorites bar.

4. **Navigate Web pages.**
   a. Open the Web page www.sportsline.com using the Address bar.
   b. Follow the links to investigate the content.
   c. Click the Home button.

5. **Get Help.**
   a. Open Microsoft Internet Explorer Help, then click the Index tab.
   b. Type "search" as your keyword.
   c. Scroll down to the entry "searching the Web" in the index list, then double-click it.
   d. In the Topics Found dialog box, double-click "Finding the information you want."
   e. Read about searching the Web.
   f. Close the Microsoft Internet Explorer Help window.

6. **Print a Web page.**
   a. Open the Web page www.buckinghamgate.com using the Address bar.
   b. Print the first page only.

7. **Search for information on the Internet.**
   a. Open the Search Assistant in the Search Explorer bar.
   b. Type any keyword or phrase for which you would like to find information, then execute the search.
   c. Explore some of the hyperlinks you find and some of the documents that open.
   d. When you finish reviewing the documents you find, close the Search Explorer bar.

8. **Exit Internet Explorer.**
   a. Exit Internet Explorer.

Independent Challenges

1. You will soon graduate with a degree in business communications. Before entering the workforce, you want to be sure that you are up to date on recent advances in your field. You decide that checking the Web will provide the most current information. In addition, you can research potential companies for employment opportunities. Use Internet Explorer to open the All Business Network home page at www.all-biz.com. Select a promising site, and then click the Print button to print the page.

2. You leave tomorrow for a business trip to Toyko, Japan. You want to be sure that you take the right clothes for the weather and decide that the best place to check weather conditions is the Web. Open two of the following weather sites to determine the weather in Toyko at this time of the year. Use the Print command to print the weather report for Tokyo from two sites.

The Weather Channel	www.weather.com
CNN Weather	www.cnn.com/WEATHER
Yahoo Weather	weather.yahoo.com

3. You work at a newspaper company, and your manager wants to buy a new desktop computer. She assigns you the task of investigating her options. You decide that using the Web is more expedient than traveling to various computer stores. Access the following computer company Web sites, and print a page from the Web site that offers the best deals on prices, service, and shipping options.

CompUSA	www.compusa.com
Apple	www.apple.com
Dell	www.dell.com

4. A recent newspaper article you read listed the URLs of some popular search engines. To compare these search engines, create a chart showing the results of searching for the word "floptical." List each search engine and the number of hits in your chart. Why do you think that each search engine provides different results?

Yahoo	www.yahoo.com
AltaVista	www.altavista.com
Excite	www.excite.com

Visual Workshop

Use the Search Assistant to find and print the Web page shown in Figure A-17. (*Hint*: Add quotation marks to your search string, for example: "NASA Observatorium Earth Science".)

FIGURE A-17

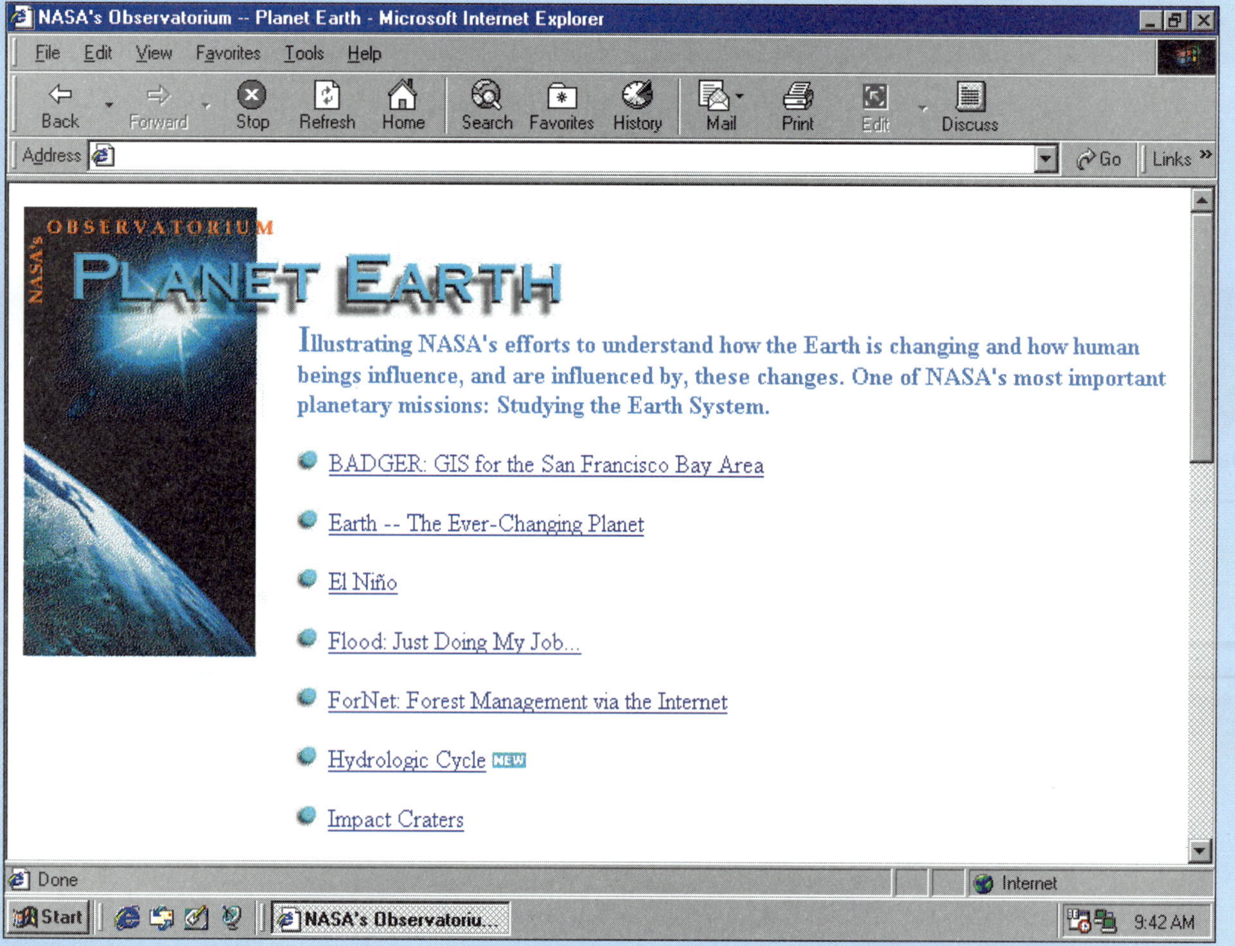

Internet | Unit B

Creating a Web Publication

Objectives

- Plan Web publication content
- Create a Web page document
- Format a Web page
- Create a Web page from a Word document
- Create a Web page from an Access table
- Create a Web page from an Excel workbook
- Create Web pages from a PowerPoint presentation
- Add hyperlinks

Microsoft Office 2000 offers features that help you create your own Web pages from scratch or convert existing Office documents to **Hypertext Markup Language** (**HTML**). HTML is the language used to describe the content and format of Web pages. Karen Rosen is the director of human resources at MediaLoft. Karen wants to create a set of Web pages that she will eventually place, or **publish**, on the MediaLoft intranet to help new MediaLoft employees learn more about employee benefits and programs. Karen will use Office 2000 to create the new Web pages.

Unit B

Internet

Planning Web Publication Content

It is important to plan your Web pages carefully before creating them. Planning is especially crucial when you are creating a **Web publication**, or a group of associated Web pages focusing on a particular theme or topic. Following a step-by-step process can help you organize tasks logically and also help to ensure that you identify and complete the necessary steps involved. Before she actually begins creating any Web pages, Karen plans their content and organization as well as the tasks involved in preparing them.

Details

In planning her Web pages Karen is careful to:

Sketch outlines of the pages

Draw a sketch of how you want each page to look, including the links between pages. Karen identifies the documents she wants to include on the intranet, sketches the layout, and adds notes, as shown in Figure B-1.

For each page, perform the following tasks:

- **Create a new document and enter the page's text, or use the Office 2000 programs to create a Web page from an existing file.**

  You can use a Web page template as a guide to create your Web page. If you want to create a Web page from an existing file, you can use the features in each Office 2000 program to convert the file to HTML for use on the Web. Karen will create a new Web page in Word and then convert several existing Office documents to HTML files.

- **Format page appearance**

  You can use Word to edit any Web page document—even those not created with Word—to apply visual themes and backgrounds and to add images. Karen will use Word's tools to enhance each page's appearance. She also will apply a common visual theme to her pages and insert the MediaLoft company logo at the top of the first page of her Web publication.

- **View pages using a Web browser**

  Confirm that your completed Web page appears as desired by viewing it in your Web browser window. If necessary, you can use Word to make corrections. Karen will view her pages in Internet Explorer to confirm their appearance.

Format hyperlinks

After finalizing the text and graphics of your Web pages, you can add hyperlinks to connect them. Karen's sketch indicates that she will eventually create links to the MediaLoft home page and to the MediaLoft Human Resources page after publishing her pages on the MediaLoft intranet.

FIGURE B-1: Karen's Web page sketch

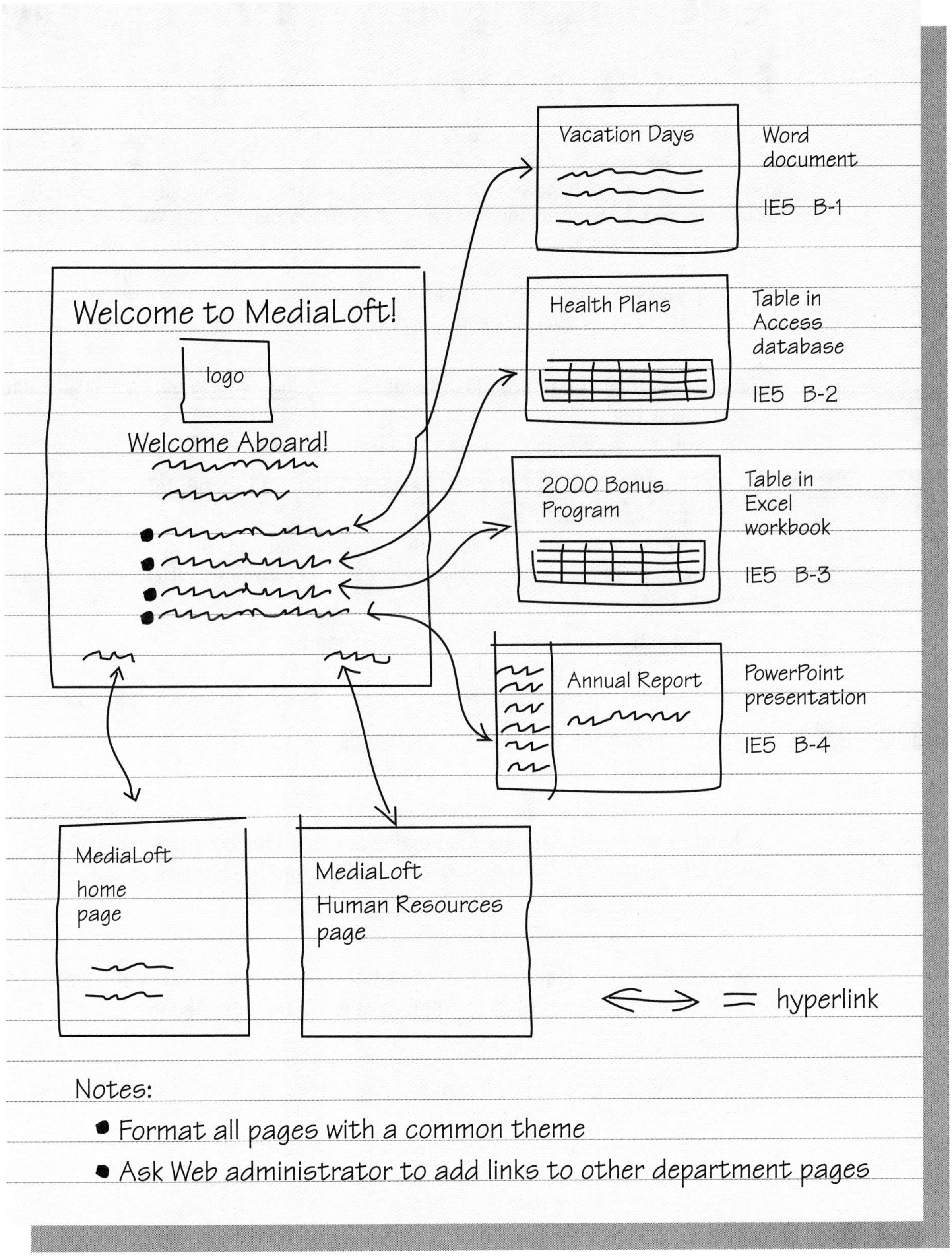

Unit B

Internet

Creating a Web Page Document

To create a Web page, you must prepare a document that uses HTML formatting. HTML places codes, called **tags**, around all the elements in your document that describe how they should appear when viewed using a Web browser. The Microsoft Office Web tools simplify this process by inserting codes for you. Additionally, the Web Pages tab, shown in Figure B-2, in Word includes templates that you can use to create your Web pages, such as a table of contents or a right-aligned column. Karen uses a Web page template in Word to create the basic structure of the MediaLoft Welcome page. When completed, the Welcome page will include links to a description of vacation days, a comparison of health plans, and other links of interest to new MediaLoft employees.

Steps

1. Start Word, then make sure the Standard and Formatting toolbars are visible and the Office Assistant is hidden
   You use the Web Pages tab to select a Web page template.
2. Click **File** on the menu bar, click **New**, click the **Web Pages tab**, then double-click the **Simple Layout icon**
   A new Web page document based on the Simple Layout template opens in your document window. Note the appearance of placeholder text, which you will delete when you add your own information.
3. Click **Format** on the menu bar, then click **Theme**
   The Theme dialog box opens and displays a list of themes that you can apply to your Web page. When you click a theme in the Choose a Theme list box, its preview appears in the dialog box.
4. In the Choose a Theme list box, click **Blends**, then click **OK**
   The Blends theme is applied to your Web page.
5. Click the **Save button** on the Standard toolbar, in the Save As dialog box click **Change Title**, in the Set Page Title dialog box type **Welcome to MediaLoft!**, click **OK**, type **Welcome** in the File name text box, make sure the location of your Project Disk is displayed in the Save in list box, then click **Save**
   The file is saved in HTML format with the HTML tags inserted. The Welcome page redisplays.
6. Select the heading **Main Heading Goes Here**, type **Welcome to MediaLoft!**, replace the heading **Section 1 Heading Goes Here** with **Welcome Aboard!**, then replace the next paragraph with the paragraph shown in Figure B-3
7. Press **[Enter]** twice, click the **Bullets button** on the Formatting toolbar, type **Number of employee vacation days**, press **[Enter]**, then repeat this procedure to enter the text for the remaining bullets shown in Figure B-3
   To add a bullet, press [Enter] when the insertion point appears at the end of a bulleted line. You will add the appropriate text for links to the other MediaLoft pages here; however, you will create the actual links later.
8. Press **[Enter]** twice, type **MediaLoft home page**, press **[Enter]**, then type **MediaLoft Human Resources page**
   You have entered all the text for the Welcome page.
9. Use the mouse pointer to select the next line of text to the end of the page, press **[Delete]**, then save and close your document

Trouble?

If you see a message saying you need to install the feature, insert your Office 2000 CD in the appropriate drive and click OK. See your instructor or technical support person for assistance.

Trouble?

If you do not have the Blends theme, or if this theme is not installed, select any other available theme and then continue with Step 5.

Trouble?

Click the More Buttons button to locate buttons that are not visible on your screen.

FIGURE B-2: Web Pages tab in New dialog box

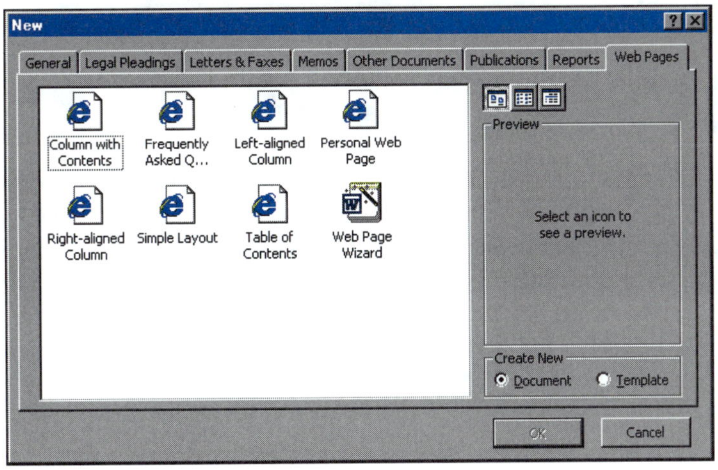

FIGURE B-3: Text entered for the Welcome page

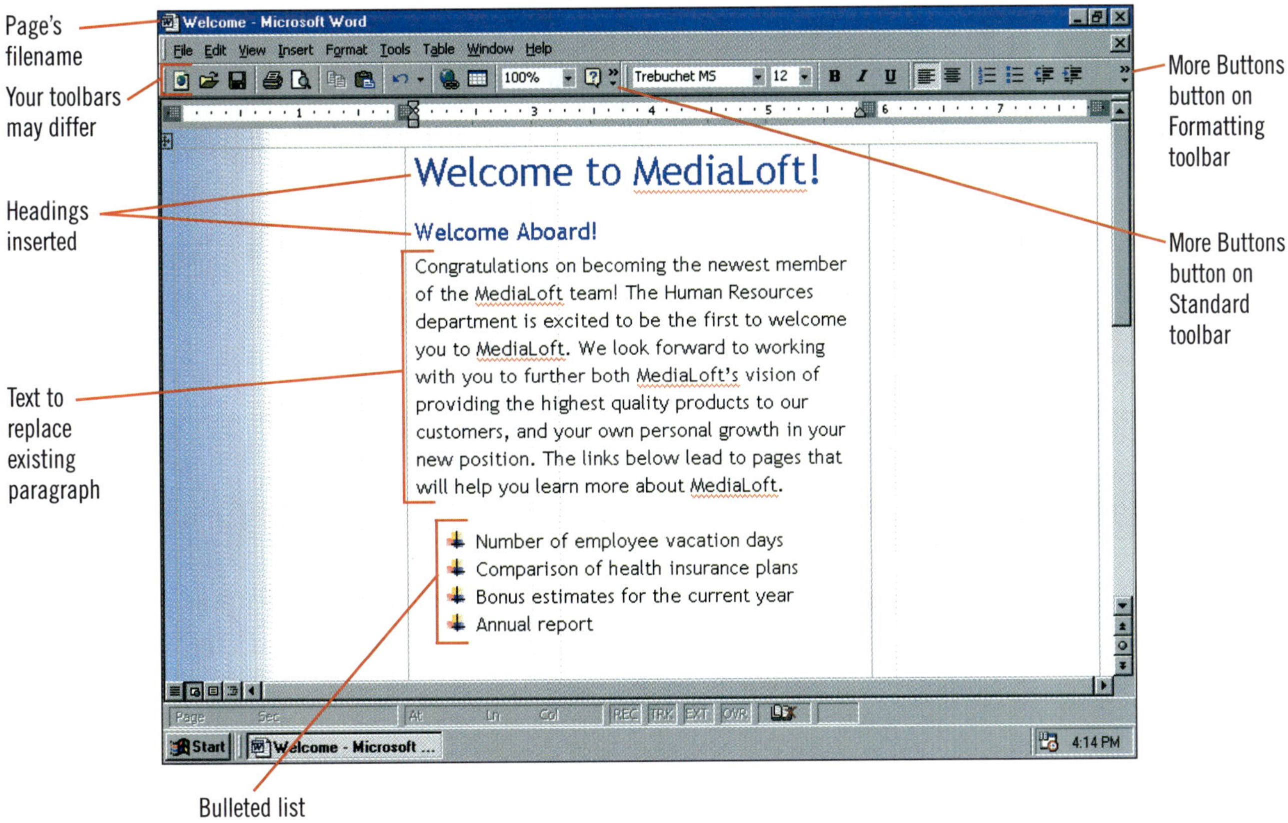

CLUES TO USE

Choosing Web page content and style

Before finalizing the appearance of your Web publication, analyze other types of Web pages. Their style, layout, and content can suggest new ideas about how to present your information. By viewing a wide variety of pages, you also might learn about Web page formatting features that have only recently become available. Remember, however, that a Web publication expresses your company's or your own identity; include personal touches rather than simply copying other pages.

Unit B

Internet

Formatting a Web Page

In addition to working with Web pages in Word, you can also create and edit Web documents in **FrontPage Express**, a program specifically designed for Web page production that is included as part of the Internet Explorer 5 suite. Like Word, FrontPage Express includes many tools and templates for creating and editing Web pages. Table B-1 lists some HTML-specific buttons available on the FrontPage Express toolbars. Although Karen likes the template and visual style she selected for her Web page, she wants to change some of its formatting and add a graphic. She uses FrontPage Express to make these changes.

Steps

Trouble?

If you cannot locate FrontPage Express, ask your instructor or technical support person for assistance.

1. Click the **Start button**, point to **Programs**, point to **Internet Explorer**, then click **FrontPage Express**
   FrontPage Express opens and a blank page appears in the document window.
2. If necessary, maximize the FrontPage Express window
3. Click the **Open button** on the Standard toolbar, in the Open File dialog box click **Browse**, make sure the location of your Project Disk is displayed in the Look in list box, then double-click **Welcome** in the file list
   The heading should be centered on the page.
4. At the top of the page, click anywhere in the heading **Welcome to MediaLoft!**, then click the **Center button** on the Formatting toolbar
5. Click anywhere in the heading **Welcome Aboard!**, click the **Change Style list arrow** on the Formatting toolbar, then click **Heading 2**
   The current heading now reflects the Heading 2 style, as shown in Figure B-4. Next you will insert the logo.
6. Click at the end of the **Welcome to MediaLoft!** line, then press **[Enter]**
   This new centered line will be the location for the MediaLoft logo.
7. Click the **Insert Image button** on the Standard toolbar, click **Browse**, make sure the location of your Project Disk is displayed in the Look in list box, click **MLoft** in the file list, then click **Open**
   The MediaLoft logo appears in the blank paragraph, as shown in Figure B-5. Usually, the final step in creating a Web page is to confirm its appearance using your Web browser. However, because your page contains only simple formatting and no advanced elements, such as tables, FrontPage Express displays the page exactly as it would appear in your browser window. Therefore, you do not need to open the page in Internet Explorer.
8. Save and close the file, then close FrontPage Express

QuickTip

The Change Style list only contains styles compatible with HTML.

FIGURE B-4: Headings and list formatted

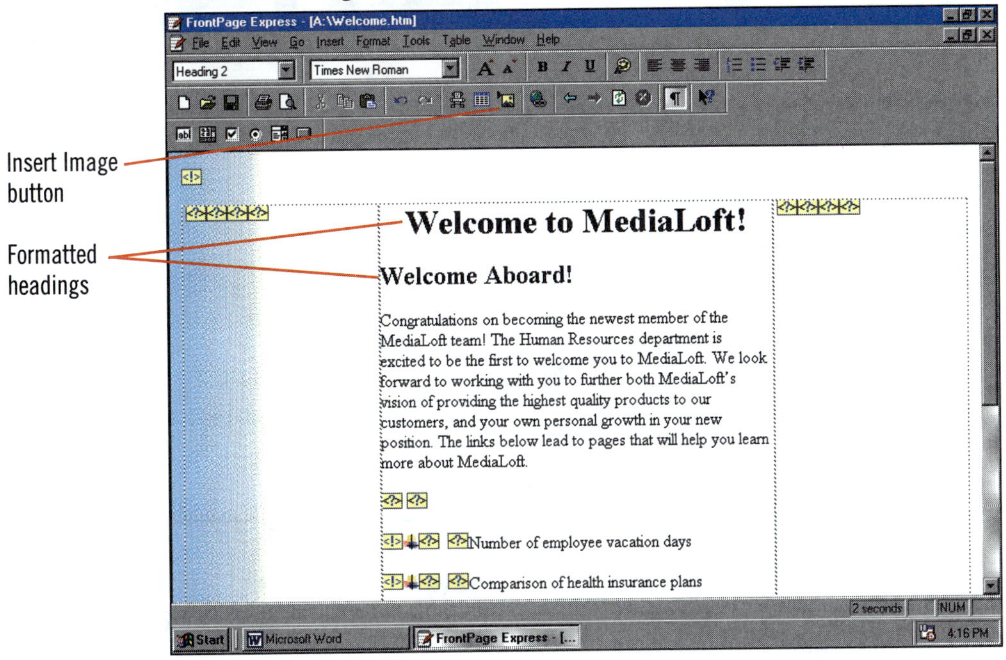

FIGURE B-5: Completed Welcome page

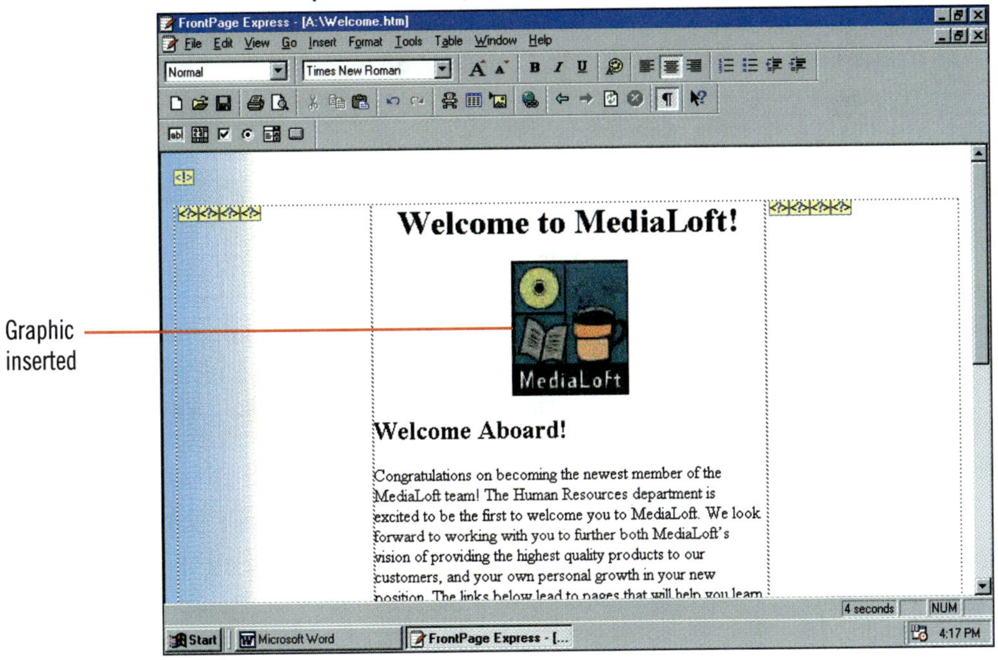

TABLE B-1: FrontPage Express formatting buttons

button	function
	Increases the font size of selected text to the next highest HTML-standard size
	Decreases the font size of selected text to the next lowest HTML-standard size
	Displays available text colors and lets you create custom colors
	Inserts an automated Web page component, such as a Java script, to perform a task automatically
	Refreshes the current page's appearance
	Inserts an existing graphic in the active document at the location of the insertion point

Unit B

Internet

Creating a Web Page from a Word Document

In addition to offering tools that help you create new Web pages, Office 2000 makes creating Web pages from existing files easy. You can use the Web features in Office to convert files from their Office formats to HTML, which is necessary to make them available on the Web. As noted in her original sketch, Karen wants to create Web pages using several of her existing Office documents. She starts by creating a Web page from a description of company vacation days stored in a Word file.

Steps

Trouble?

If the file IE5 B-1 does not appear in the list of files on your Project Disk in the Open dialog box, change the Files of type list box to display "All Files" or "All Word Documents."

1. In Word, open the file **IE5 B-1** from your Project Disk
   The file contains a description of the number of vacation days for MediaLoft employees.
2. Click **File** on the menu bar, then click **Save as Web Page**
   The Save As dialog box opens. In order to save a Web page, you need to specify its filename and page title.
3. Click **Change Title**, in the Set Page Title dialog box type **Vacation Days**, click **OK**, in the File name text box type **Vacation**, make sure the location of your Project Disk is displayed in the Save in list box, then click **Save**
   Word saves a copy of the document in HTML format and switches to Web Layout view. Now you can change some of the page's formatting.

Trouble?

If the Style list arrow or the Center button do not appear on your Formatting toolbar, click the More Buttons button to display additional toolbar buttons.

4. Select the heading **Vacation Days**, click the **Style list arrow** on the Formatting toolbar, click **Heading 1**, click the **Center button** on the Formatting toolbar, press **[Ctrl][End]** to move the insertion point to the end of the document, press **[Enter]**, then type **Return to Welcome page**
   Your Vacation Days Web page should match Figure B-6. "Vacation" appears in the title bar because Word automatically uses the filename as the Web page title instead of the page title that you entered in Step 3. In Internet Explorer, the page's title will appear in the title bar. Next you decide to add a theme to the new page that matches the Welcome page; you will format the "Return to Welcome page" text as a hyperlink later in this unit.
5. Click **Format** on the menu bar, click **Theme**, in the Choose a Theme list box click **Blends** (or the style that you selected in the previous lesson), then click **OK**
   The Blends theme is applied to the Web page, as shown in Figure B-7. Your completed Vacation Days Web page now matches the appearance of the Welcome page you created.
6. Save the Vacation Days Web page, then close it

CLUES TO USE

Web browsers and Web page appearance

When you use a browser other than Internet Explorer 5, such as Netscape Navigator or Lynx (a text-only browser), remember that the appearance of your Web pages might differ. Depending on your browser's options, you can change settings, such as always using a certain font or selecting a certain window size, that affect the appearance of Web pages. Using common fonts and simple backgrounds is one way to ensure that the appearance of your Web pages is consistent between browsers.

FIGURE B-6: Vacation Days Web page

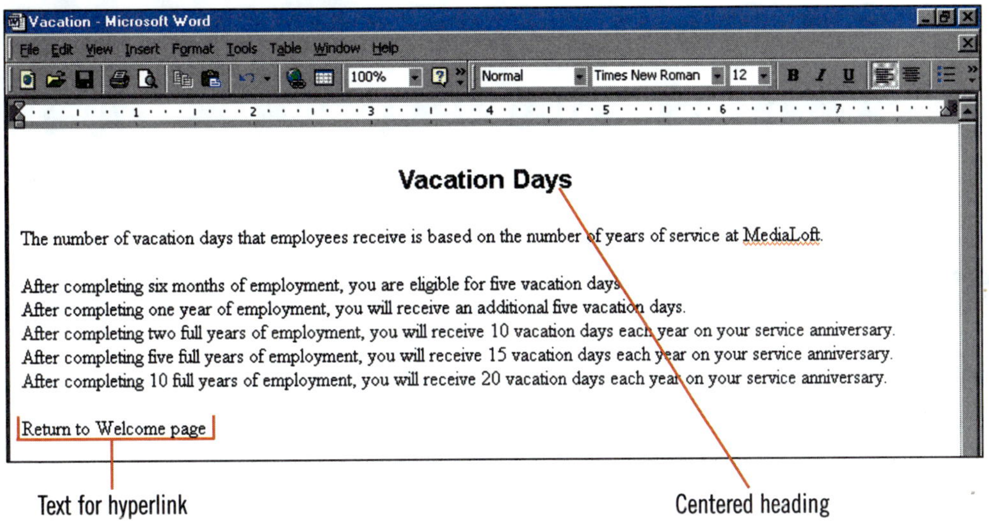

FIGURE B-7: Completed Vacation Days Web page

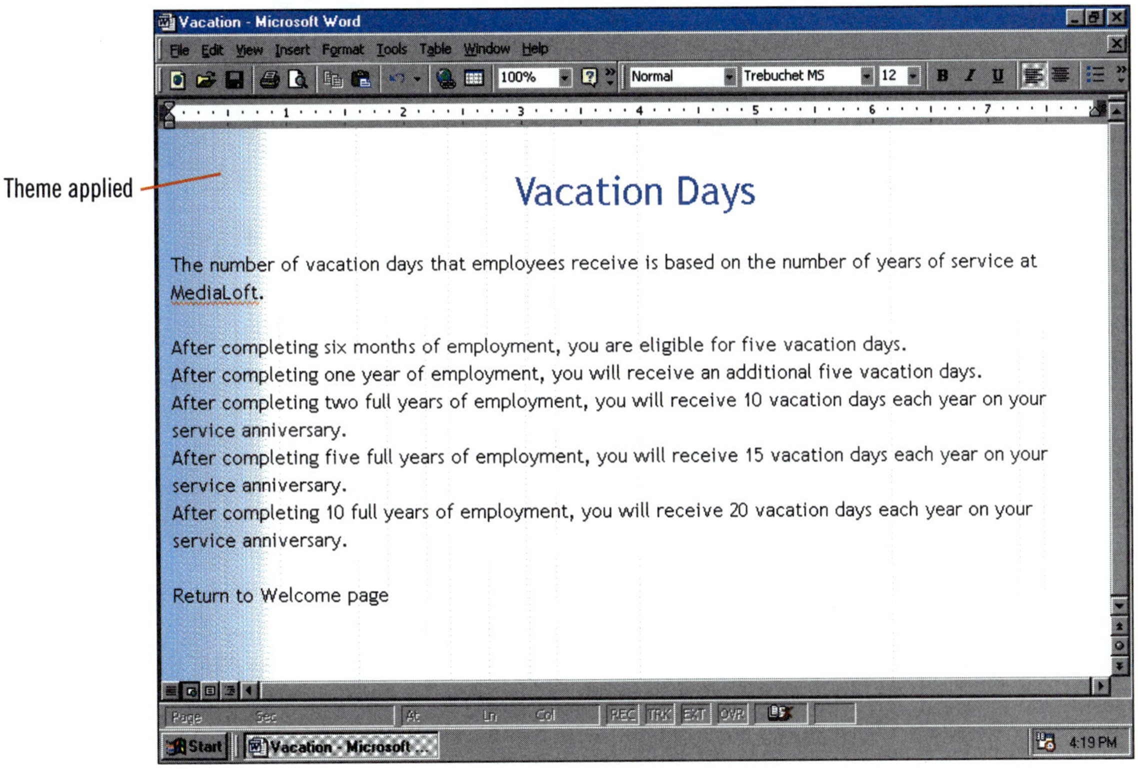

Internet

Unit B

Internet

Creating a Web Page from an Access Table

Like Word, Access offers a tool for converting existing files to Web pages. You can save each element of a database that you select as a separate HTML file. Then you can use Word to format the HTML file. Karen wants to create a Web page that contains a table comparing various health insurance plans available to MediaLoft employees. This information is currently stored in an Access database table.

Steps

Trouble?

If the Office Assistant appears, hide it.

1. Start Access, open the file **IE5 B-2** from your Project Disk, then click **Tables** on the Objects bar in the IE5 B-2 Database window
   The Health Plans table is selected automatically. You will export the table to HTML and then edit it using Word.

2. Click **File** on the menu bar, then click **Export**
   The Export Table 'Health Plans' To dialog box opens, as shown in Figure B-8. You have the option of exporting only the data, in which case you just click Save, or you can export the data and the table format.

3. Click the **Save as type list arrow**, click **HTML Documents**, click the **Save formatted check box**, then click **Save**
   The HTML Output Options dialog box opens. Access needs an existing HTML document on which to base the exported table. You will use the Template file on your Project Disk as an output sample.

4. Press **[Delete]** to delete the current text, click **Browse**, click the file **Template** on your Project Disk, click **OK**, then click **OK**
   After a few moments, the table is exported.

Trouble?

If a dialog box asking if you want to make Word your default Web page editor opens, click No.

5. Close Access, open the file **Health Plans** in Word, click **Format** on the menu bar, click **Theme**, in the Choose a Theme list box click **Blends**, then click **OK**
   The theme is applied as shown in Figure B-9.

6. Press **[Ctrl][End]** to scroll to the bottom of the table, press **[Enter]**, then type **Return to Welcome page**
   Notice that the fonts used on the page are different. You can select all text and then apply the theme's Normal style to it to make the fonts consistent.

7. Press **[Ctrl][A]** to select the entire page, click the **Style list arrow** on the Formatting toolbar, click **Normal**, then click anywhere outside the table to deselect it
   The page appears as shown in Figure B-10; the same font style is applied to all text. Later in this unit you will format the hyperlink text to link to the Welcome page.

8. Save your changes, then close the file in Word

CLUES TO USE

Static and dynamic pages

You can use Access to create static and dynamic Web pages. A **static HTML page** only contains the current information in the table that you are converting. A **dynamic HTML page**, on the other hand, links your Web page to the original database file that you used to create it. When you change the original object in the database, the content of a dynamic page changes to reflect your updates, while the contents of a static page will remain unchanged. Use a dynamic Web page if you expect to change your original Access object often. However, to use this feature, you must locate the database file containing the object on the same file server that contains the dynamic Web page.

FIGURE B-8: Export Table 'Health Plans' To dialog box

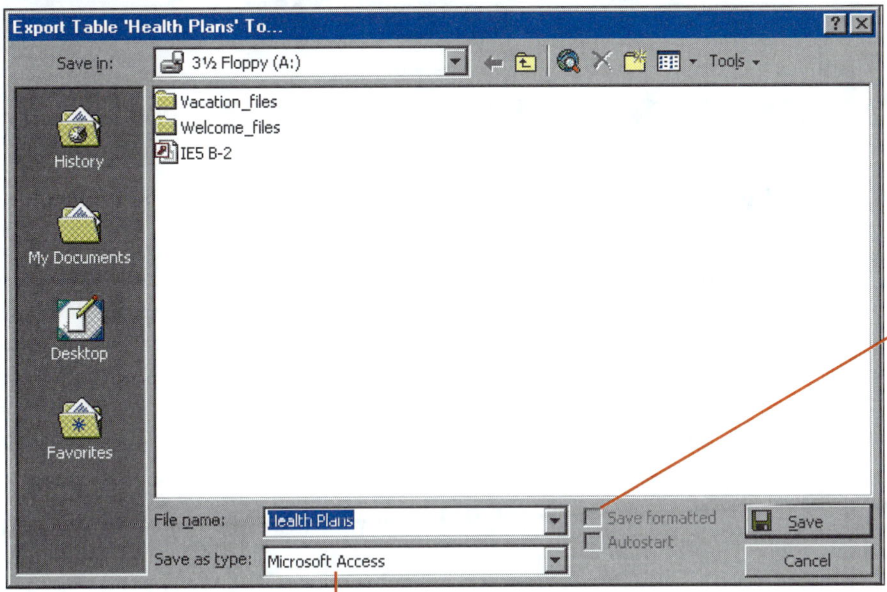

FIGURE B-9: Health Plans Web page in Word

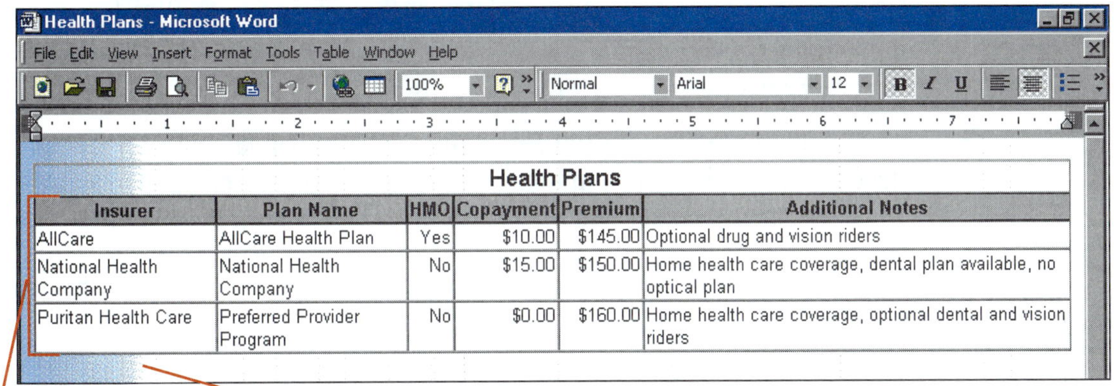

FIGURE B-10: Completed Health Plans Web page

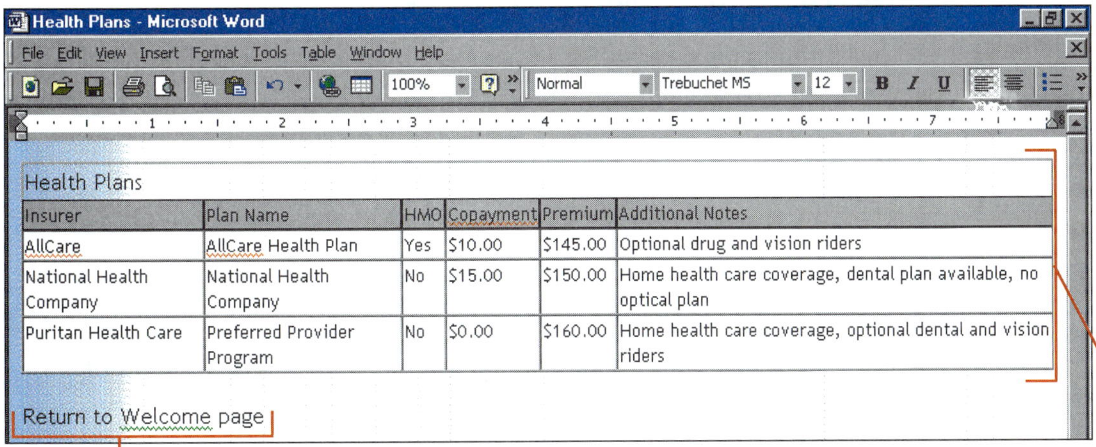

Internet

Unit B

Internet

Creating a Web Page from an Excel Workbook

Like Word and Access, you can create Web pages using existing Excel files. However, Excel lets you select specific worksheet ranges to use as sources for Web pages, instead of having to include all of the worksheets or cells in an entire workbook. Karen wants to add another Web page to the Welcome publication. Titled 2000 Bonus Program, this page will highlight MediaLoft's bonus program estimates for the year. Karen creates this page from an Excel workbook to show the estimated bonus percentages for employees by quarter and department.

Steps

Trouble?

If the Office Assistant appears, hide it.

1. Start Excel, open the file **IE5 B-3** from your Project Disk, click and drag to select the range **A1:G7**, click **File** on the menu bar, then click **Save as Web Page**
   The Save As dialog box opens. As with Access, you use this dialog box in Excel to specify the Web page's filename and title.
2. Click the **Selection: $A$1:$G$7 option button** in the Save As dialog box, click **Change Title**, in the Set Title dialog box type **2000 Bonus Program**, click **OK**, in the File name text box type **Bonus**, click **Save**, then close Excel without saving changes to the file IE5 B-3
   Now view and edit your new HTML file in Word.

Trouble?

If you do not see the Bonus file, click the Files of type list arrow, then click All Files. If the file opens in Excel, close Excel, then repeat Step 3. Make sure you click the Open in Microsoft Word option to open the file correctly.

3. In Word, click the **Open button** on the Standard toolbar, click the **Bonus** file, click the **Open button list arrow** in the Open dialog box, then click **Open in Microsoft Word**
   The 2000 Bonus Program Web page opens in Word, as shown in Figure B-11. You will add the theme and then delete the first row of the table because it repeats the page's title. You also will add text at the bottom of the page to use as a hyperlink, and then change the columns so their widths are equal.
4. Click **Format** on the menu bar, click **Theme**, in the Choose a Theme list box click **Blends**, then click **OK**

Trouble?

If you see Delete Cells on the pop-up menu instead of Delete Rows, click Delete Cells, click the Delete entire row option button, then click OK.

5. Select the first row of the table (which contains the repeated heading), right-click the selected row, on the pop-up menu click **Delete Rows**, press **[Ctrl][End]**, press **[Enter]**, then type **Return to Welcome page**
6. Select the table, click **Table** on the menu bar, point to **AutoFit**, then click **Distribute Columns Evenly**
7. With the table still selected, click the **Style list arrow** on the Formatting toolbar, click **Normal**, then click anywhere outside the table to deselect it
   Now the table and the Web page have the same theme and font style as the other pages in the Web, as shown in Figure B-12.
8. Save your changes, click **Yes** to overwrite the file, then close the file
9. Click in Word, click **Bonus** in the file list, click the **Open button list arrow**, click **Open in Browser**, then view your completed 2000 Bonus Program Web page
   The page opens in Internet Explorer, as shown in Figure B-13.

FIGURE B-11: 2000 Bonus Program Web page in Word

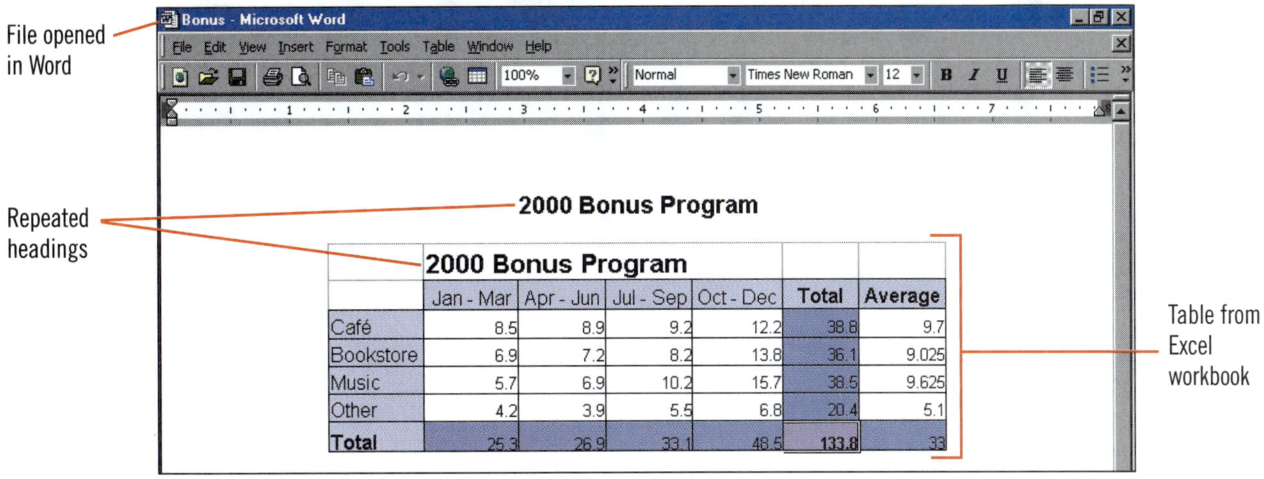

FIGURE B-12: Completed 2000 Bonus Program Web page

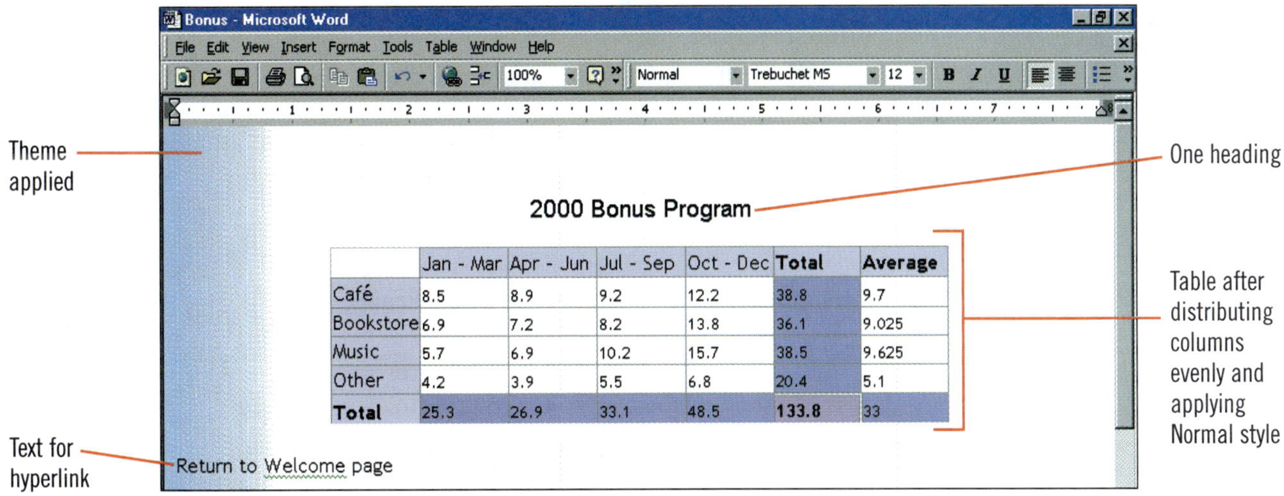

FIGURE B-13: Web page in Internet Explorer

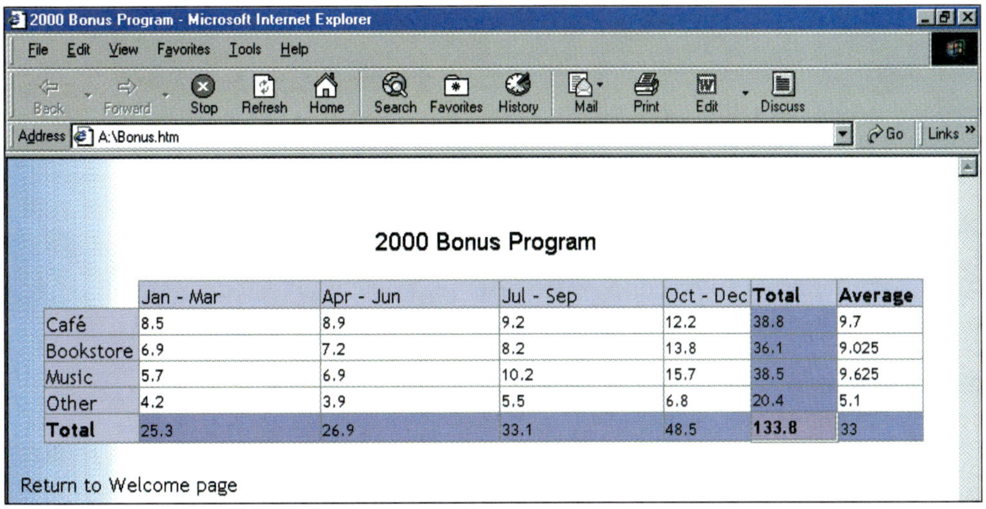

Internet

Unit B

Internet

Creating Web Pages from a PowerPoint Presentation

Unlike other Office files, PowerPoint presentations contain multiple screens of information, called slides. When you convert a PowerPoint presentation to HTML format, PowerPoint creates a separate page for each slide and groups the pages in a folder. When viewing your presentation on the Web, your audience can then navigate through it much like they would in PowerPoint. Karen wants to convert a PowerPoint presentation containing six slides from the company's annual report to HTML format. The presentation outlines the company's recent accomplishments and immediate goals.

Steps

Trouble?

If the Office Assistant appears, hide it.

Trouble?

It might take several minutes to save the file.

Trouble?

Click the More Buttons buttons on the Standard and Formatting toolbars to locate buttons that are not visible on your toolbars.

1. Start PowerPoint, open the file **IE5 B-4** from your Project Disk, then use the slide navigation buttons to view the presentation
   The presentation's six slides outline the company's accomplishments and goals.
2. Click **File** on the menu bar, click **Save as Web Page**, click **Change Title**, in the Set Page Title dialog box type **Annual Report**, click **OK**, in the File name text box type **Annual**, then click **Save**
   Because PowerPoint creates a group of Web pages, you could consider the Web pages based on this presentation as a publication within your publication. PowerPoint exports the current presentation to HTML format. Preview the PowerPoint presentation in your Web browser.
3. Click **File** on the menu bar, then click **Web Page Preview**
   The presentation opens in Internet Explorer, as shown in Figure B-14. You can click a page title in the left frame to open that page, or click the arrows that appear to the right and left of the "Slide 1 of 6" text at the bottom of the window to view the slides.
4. Click the **PowerPoint program button**, click I at the end of the **1999** line on the title slide, press **[Enter]** twice, click the **Decrease Font Size button** on the Formatting toolbar three times, then type **Return to Welcome page**
   The title page now contains a link back to the Welcome page. Because your PowerPoint Web publication is a group of pages instead of a single page, you must use PowerPoint to create the actual link, whereas in the other Office files you can create all of your links in Word.
5. Select the text **Return to Welcome page**, click the **Insert Hyperlink button** on the Standard toolbar, in the Browse for section click **File**, then double-click the **Welcome** file on your Project Disk
6. Click **OK** in the Insert Hyperlink dialog box, then save your changes
   The hyperlink is now created; you will test the link in the next lesson.
7. Click **File** on the menu bar, then click **Web Page Preview** and view your presentation
   Internet Explorer displays the first slide from the presentation, as well as navigation tools for the remaining slides in frames, as shown in Figure B-15.
8. Close Internet Explorer and PowerPoint

FIGURE B-14: PowerPoint presentation in Internet Explorer

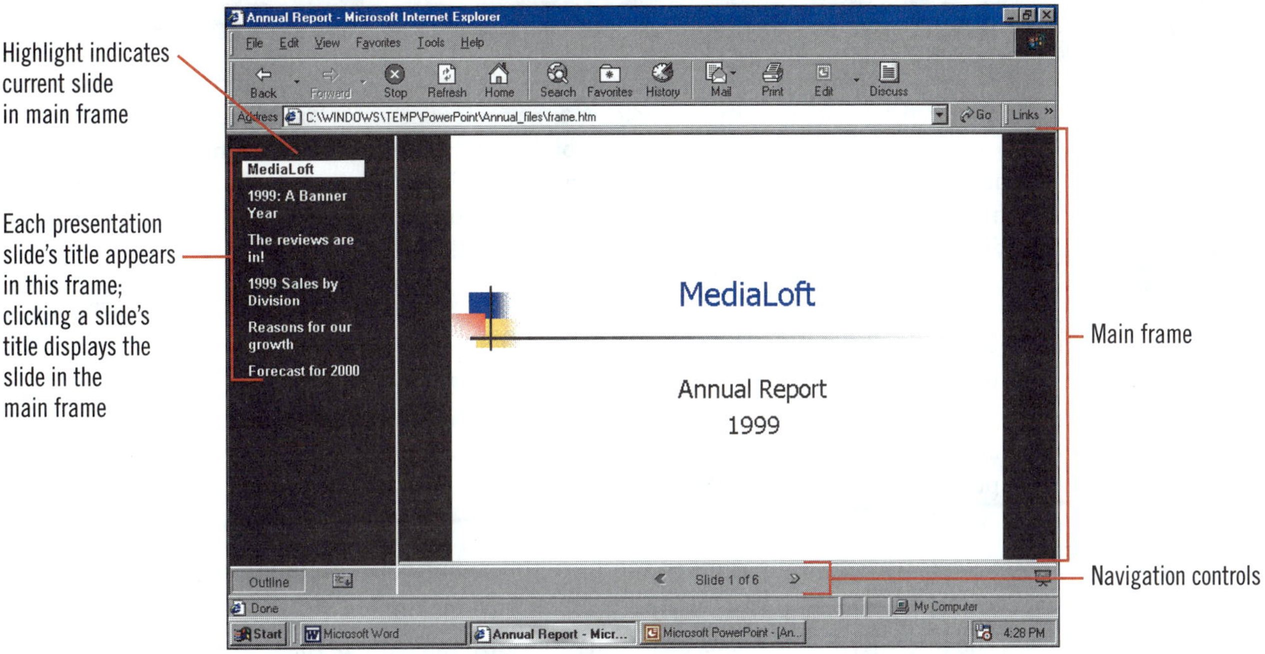

FIGURE B-15: Presentation title slide with hyperlink added

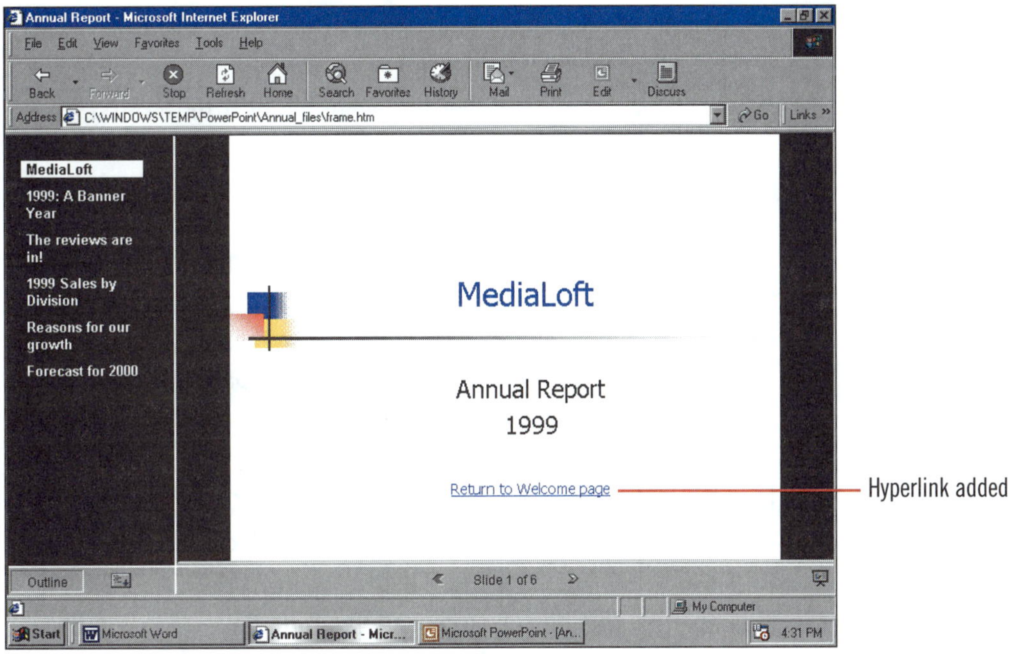

CLUES TO USE

Using frames

Frames help you to navigate a group of associated Web pages. Frame formatting is most useful when you want to use common navigation elements for all pages. Although frames are convenient, remember that not all Web browsers support them. A popular way to address this problem is to create two versions of a publication—one with frames and one without—and to offer a choice between the two on the publication's home page. If time or resources limit you to one version, then base your decision on your audience's capabilities. For example, if you create a page for a company intranet and know that every computer has the latest version of a browser installed, adding frames to your publication makes sense. However, if you create a page for a Web publication and want the largest possible audience, choosing frames excludes some users from viewing your document.

Unit B

Internet

Adding Hyperlinks

After you create your page, you need to add hyperlinks both between publication pages and to other Web pages to make it easy for your audience to navigate your pages. You can use hyperlinks to navigate between unpublished documents or published Web pages. Karen's sketch shows links from her Welcome page to each associated page as well as a link back to the Welcome page from each associated page. Eventually, she will add the links on the Welcome page to take users to other MediaLoft pages of interest. She starts by adding the links to her Welcome page.

Steps 1 2 3 4

QuickTip

Absolute links, which contain only a fixed address, are used when you don't want the addresses of your links to change at all.

Trouble?

Click the More Buttons button on the Standard toolbar to locate buttons that are not visible on your toolbar.

Trouble?

Word has a minor error that could delete the bullets on your Web page and the theme when you view the page in the browser. The procedure in Step 6 corrects this problem.

QuickTip

You already created the hyperlink in your PowerPoint presentation.

1. Open the **Welcome** file from your Project Disk in Word, then if necessary, scroll down until you see all of the bulleted items in the document window
   Next you create the links to the associated pages using **relative links**, or links that give another page's address in relation to the current page. Once you complete the links, you can publish the pages to the Web in their current directory structure, and the links will remain accurate.
2. Select the text to the right of the first bullet, but not the bullet itself, then click the **Insert Hyperlink button** on the Standard toolbar
   The Insert Hyperlink dialog box opens, as shown in Figure B-16.
3. In the Browse for section click **File**, double-click the **Vacation** file on your Project Disk, then click **OK** in the Insert Hyperlink dialog box to close it
   The text beside the first bullet changes to underlined text, indicating it is now a hyperlink.
4. Move the mouse pointer over the hyperlink next to the first bullet
   As shown in Figure B-17, the mouse pointer changes to , indicating that this text is a hyperlink. The linked page's path and filename appears above the link. Now you can use the Welcome page to finish the remaining pages.
5. Repeat Steps 2 through 3 to create relative links for the remaining lines of bulleted text—link the second bullet to the Health Plans file, link the third bullet to the Bonus file, link the fourth bullet to the Annual file, then save the Welcome file
   Your final tasks are to add a link to the Welcome page at the bottom of each associated page and to check all the links you have inserted.
6. Click the first bullet character in the list to select it, press **[Delete]** twice, repeat this for each bullet, click **Format** on the menu bar, click **Theme**, in the Choose a Theme list box click **Blends**, click **OK**, then click the **Save button** on the Standard toolbar
   Now the bullets and the theme will be displayed correctly in the browser.
7. Click the link **Number of employee vacation days**, click the **Edit button** in Internet Explorer, select the text **Return to Welcome page** in the Word document that opens, click , click **File**, double-click **Welcome**, click **OK**, then save and close your document
   Now the Vacation Days Web page contains a hyperlink to return to the Welcome page.
8. Save your changes, close **Word**, click the **Back button** on the Internet Explorer toolbar, then repeat Step 7 to add the hyperlink back to the Welcome page on the rest of your Web pages
9. Save the **Welcome** file in Word, use the hyperlinks in your Web site in Internet Explorer to view the pages, then close Internet Explorer and Word
   You have successfully created and tested the links between the files in your Web publication.

FIGURE B-16: Insert Hyperlink dialog box

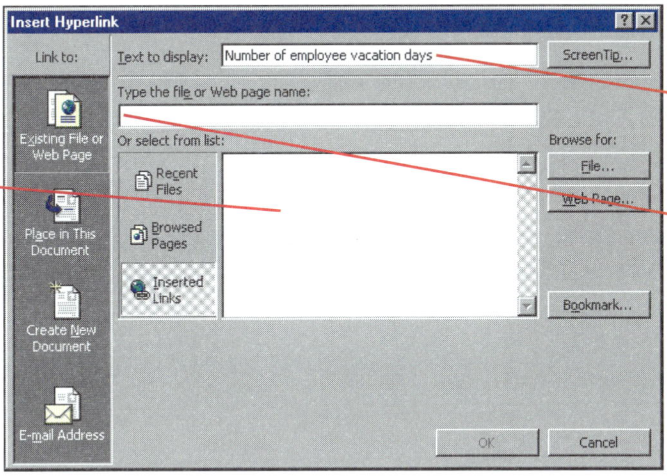

FIGURE B-17: Welcome page with hyperlink added

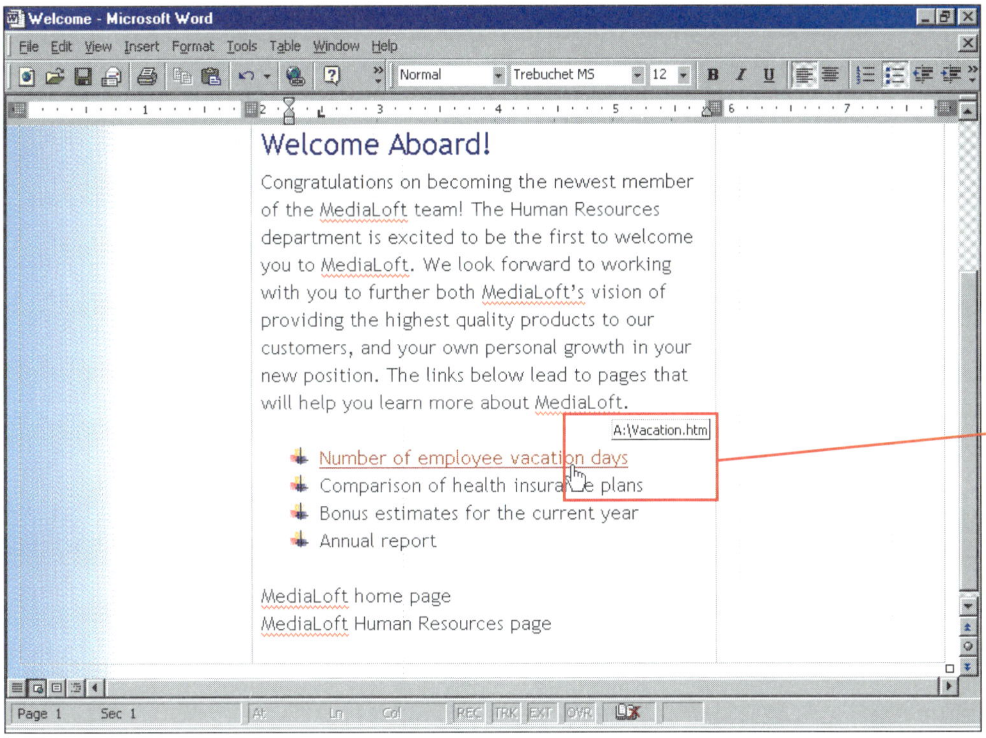

Publishing your Web pages

Your Web publication is not available to anyone outside your local computer network or workgroup until you publish it, either by placing a copy on the Web or an on intranet server. Remember that links that you create on your home page are one-way: they help users viewing your page to find other interesting pages but do not help locate your page in the first place. Try the following to advertise your Web publication: ask friends and colleagues to create links to your home page on their pages; ask the administrator of your server to add your home page to the index of the site's Web pages; or e-mail information about your publication to groups, organizations, or people with Web sites. To publish effectively on an intranet, send a memo to employees who you think might be interested in your page or ask the network administrator and the owners of other relevant pages to add links to your publication on their pages.

Internet

Practice

▶ Concepts Review

Label each element of the FrontPage Express window shown in Figure B-18.

FIGURE B-18

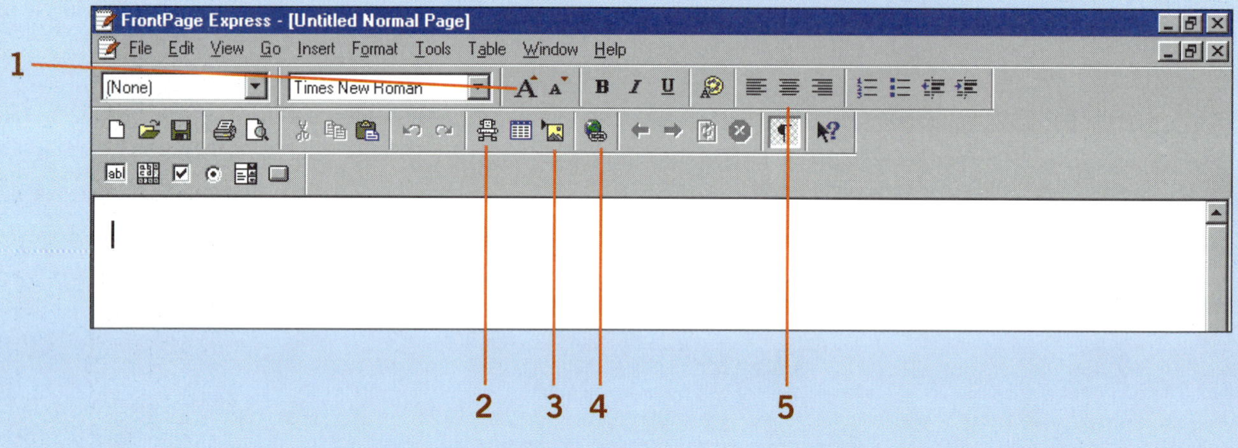

Match each term with the statement that describes it.

6. Frames
7. HTML
8. Home page
9. Dynamic page
10. FrontPage Express

a. Language for describing Web page contents and formats
b. Page linked to original database file
c. Web page editing tool
d. A format that creates borders between screen elements
e. First page of a Web publication

Select the best answer from the list of choices.

11. Frames are most useful for

- **a.** Navigating a group of associated Web pages.
- **b.** Creating hyperlinks.
- **c.** Formatting headings.
- **d.** Creating a home page.

12. Once you've created Web pages, they become available to users outside your local network only

- **a.** If you save them on your hard drive.
- **b.** After you format them.
- **c.** If you publish the pages on a Web or intranet server.
- **d.** If you use frames.

13. The final step in creating a Web publication is

- **a.** Viewing each page and making final corrections.
- **b.** Formatting hyperlinks.
- **c.** Creating Web pages based on existing files.
- **d.** Creating a home page.

14. To add a theme to a Web page in Word, you

- **a.** Click , select the theme, then click OK.
- **b.** Click , select the theme, then click Apply.
- **c.** Click Format on the menu bar, click Theme, select the theme, then click OK.
- **d.** Cannot add a theme to a Web page in Word.

Skills Review

1. Plan Web publication content.

a. Sketch an outline of a Web publication for the MediaLoft sales department, including a home page, a recent letter sent to past customers, a table of contact information for past customers, a table of the most recent sales figures, and a presentation on MediaLoft's cafe.

b. Draw arrows on your sketch indicating hyperlinks between the pages in your publication.

2. Create a Web page document.

a. Start Word.

b. Create a new document using the Table of Contents Web page template. (*Hint*: You may need to install the feature.)

c. Add the Blends theme, then save the document on your Project Disk using the filename "TOC" and the Web page title "MediaLoft Sales Department." (If you don't have this theme, select one that you do have.)

d. Change the main heading to "Sales Information," then change the first section heading to "Company Vision."

e. Replace the paragraph beneath the first section heading with the following text: To provide the highest quality publications possible for our customers.

f. Change the second section heading to: Use these links to access the latest information about MediaLoft.

g. Replace the text under the second section heading with a bulleted list containing the following items: Letter accompanying survey sent to past customers, Customer list, Most recent sales figures, and Café division overview presentation.

h. Change the third section heading to "Research."

i. Add the following bullets under the Research heading: MediaLoft home page and MediaLoft New Employee Orientation.

j. Delete the rest of the text on the page. Save your changes, then close the file.

3. Format a Web page.

a. Start FrontPage Express, then open the TOC file from your Project Disk.

b. Apply the Heading 3 style to the "Company Vision" heading, apply the Heading 2 style to the company vision statement, click to the left of the "C" in the line "Company Vision," then press [Enter].

c. Insert the MediaLoft graphic (MLoft.jpg) from your Project Disk on the blank line you created.

d. Save your changes, then close the file and FrontPage Express.

e. Open Internet Explorer, click File on the menu bar, click Open, click Browse, click the TOC file on your Project Disk, click Open, then click OK. Review the appearance of your Web page in the browser window.

4. Create a Web page from a Word document.

a. Open the file IE5 B-5 from your Project Disk in Word.

b. Save the file as a Web page with the page title "Customer Survey Letter" and the filename "Survey."

c. Add the Blends theme to the page.

d. Delete the three lines for customer address information and the blank paragraph that follows it, and then delete the text block beginning with "Very truly yours," to the end of the document.

e. Type "Return to MediaLoft home page" at the end of the document.

f. Apply the Heading 2 style to the first line of the document, then center it.

g. Save your changes to the Customer Survey Letter page, then close it.

5. **Create a Web page from an Access table.**
   a. Start Access and then open the file IE5 B-6 from your Project Disk.
   b. Export the Customers table as a formatted HTML document. Use the filename "Customers", and the Template file as an HTML document output sample.
   c. Apply the Blends theme to the page.
   d. Scroll to the bottom of the table, then type "Return to MediaLoft home page." Change the text on the page to use the theme's Normal style.
   e. Save your changes, close the file, then close Access.

6. **Create a Web page from an Excel workbook.**
   a. Start Excel, and then open the file IE5 B-7 from your Project Disk.
   b. Click and drag to select the range A1 to H6, then save the selected range as a Web page with the filename "Regions" and the page title "MediaLoft Regions Monthly Sales."
   c. Close Excel without saving changes, then open the Regions file in Word. Delete the table's heading (the one without the colored background).
   d. Apply the Blends theme to the page.
   e. At the end of the document, type "Return to MediaLoft home page."
   f. Save your changes, click Yes to overwrite the file, then close the file.

7. **Create Web pages from a PowerPoint presentation.**
   a. Start PowerPoint, open the file IE5 B-8 from your Project Disk, then use the slide navigation buttons to page through the presentation quickly.
   b. Create a hyperlink to return to the MediaLoft home page on the title slide. The Web address is http://www.course.com/Illustrated/MediaLoft.
   c. Save the presentation as a Web page with the title "Eastern Division Report" and the filename "Eastern" on your Project Disk.
   d. Preview the presentation in your browser window.
   e. Navigate the slides in Internet Explorer, then close the file and PowerPoint.

8. **Add hyperlinks.**
   a. In Word, open the file TOC.htm from your Project Disk, then scroll down if necessary so you can see the bulleted lists in the document window.
   b. Create hyperlinks for each of the bulleted items in the second section heading to the appropriate Web pages that you created in the previous steps.
   c. Create hyperlinks in the documents that you created so the "Return to MediaLoft home page" link opens the Web page with the address http://www.course.com/Illustrated/MediaLoft when clicked. Return to the TOC file, then create a hyperlink using the "MediaLoft New Employee Orientation" link that opens the Employee.htm page on your Project Disk. (*Hint:* If you make a mistake and link the wrong file to a hyperlink, right-click the hyperlink, point to Edit Hyperlink, click Remove Hyperlink, then create the hyperlink again.)
   d. Use the procedure you learned in the "Adding Hyperlinks" lesson to reapply the bullets and theme, then save the TOC file.
   e. Print the first page of each of your Web pages using the Print button in Internet Explorer, then close Word and Internet Explorer.

Independent Challenges

WEB WORK

1. You are a volunteer at the Safe Haven Emergency Shelter for families in crisis. Knowing that you have experience creating Web publications, staff members mention that they want to put information about their services and resource requests on the Internet and ask you to create pages for them using existing files for their printed materials.

To complete this independent challenge:

a. Sketch the Safe Haven Web publication. In addition to a home page, the publication should include a list of items sought for donation, a table detailing the programs the shelter offers, a chart showing last year's income and expenses, and a presentation summarizing the shelter's recent activities and immediate goals. Be sure to include links between the pages.

b. Create a home page for Safe Haven using the Simple Layout template and the Passport theme. (If you do not have this theme, select one that you do have.) Use "Safe Haven Emergency Shelter" as the heading, and create a brief mission statement, or summary of the shelter's function (to help families survive homelessness and domestic violence) to replace the sample paragraph. Create a "More About Us" section heading, and then create appropriate text for links to associated pages on the topics Making Donations, Shelter Programs, Financial Report, and Year in Review. Delete other template text as necessary. Create a third section named "Related Pages," and then create a bulleted list of hyperlinks with the names of national or local organizations whose missions are similar to Safe Haven's. (Search the Web to find organization names if necessary.) Save your home page as "Home" on your Project Disk with the page title "Safe Haven Home Page."

c. Create a Web page from the Word file IE5 B-9 from your Project Disk. Save your Web page as "Donations" with a page title of "Safe Haven Donations," and then apply the Passport theme. Change the appearance of the Web page as necessary, and be sure to insert text at the bottom of the page for a link back to the home page. Save your changes, then close the file.

d. Create a formatted Web page from the Programs table in the Access database IE5 B-10 from your Project Disk using the Template HTML file on your Project Disk. Apply the Passport theme. Distribute the table's columns evenly and then apply the Normal style (from the theme) to the cells. Add a hyperlink to return to the home page. Save your changes, close the file, then close Access.

e. Create a Web page from the range A1:F20 in the Excel workbook IE5 B-11 from your Project Disk. Save the range as a Web page named "Report" and titled "Financial Report." Close Excel without saving changes, and then open the Report file in Word. Apply the Passport theme, and then format the page as necessary so the table is easy to read. Make sure the page has only one heading; delete table rows if necessary. Be sure to insert text for a link to the home page. Save your changes and click Yes to overwrite the existing file. Close the file.

f. Create a Web page named "Goals" and titled "Annual Report" from the PowerPoint presentation file IE5 B-12 from your Project Disk. Create a hyperlink on the title slide to return to the home page. Save your changes, and then close the file and PowerPoint.

g. Add link addresses to the bulleted list of links on your home page, and then test the links while adding the return links from each of the associated pages. Use the procedure you learned in the "Adding Hyperlinks" lesson to reapply the bullets and theme, then save the Home file. Save your changes, then preview your documents in Internet Explorer.

h. Print the first page of each of your Web pages using Internet Explorer, then close Internet Explorer and Word.

WEB WORK

2. You work in the public relations office at Fox Oil Corporation. Recognizing public concern following recent oil spills by other companies, Fox Oil wants to publicize the steps it is taking to guard against oil-tanker spills. Your supervisor asks you to adapt documents created for print and television ad campaigns to create a Web publication for Fox's Internet site.

To complete this independent challenge:

a. Files you will adapt include a press release, a table of Fox's oil-spill prevention programs, a table summarizing recent oil spills by company, and a presentation detailing Fox's oil-spill record and the steps it is taking to ensure that no future spills occur. Sketch how this Web publication should look. Be sure to indicate links between the home page and associated documents.

b. Create a home page for the oil-spill publication. Use an appropriate template and theme. Enter text for the home page, format it, then save the file as "Fox Home" with the title "Fox Oil Home Page" on your Project Disk. Include text for a link to the Fox Oil corporate home page, and add the Fox company logo located in the file Fox.jpg on your Project Disk. (*Hint:* To insert the logo in Word, place the insertion point in the correct location, click Insert on the menu bar, point to Picture, click From File, and then open your Project Disk and insert the Fox.jpg file. You might need to resize the logo after inserting it to make it fit. Select the image and then use the resize handles to decrease the image's size.) Save and close the file.

c. Convert the Word document IE5 B-13 on your Project Disk to HTML using the filename "Press" and the title "Press Release;" add, delete, and format the text as necessary; apply a theme; and make other necessary changes. Create a hyperlink to return to the Fox home page. Save your changes, then close the file.

d. Convert the Prevention Programs table in the Access database IE5 B-14 on your Project Disk to a formatted HTML document using the Template HTML file on your Project Disk. Edit the resulting Web page as necessary, apply a theme, and make other appropriate changes. Create a hyperlink to return to the Fox home page. Save your changes, close the file, and then close Access.

e. Convert the table in the Excel spreadsheet IE5 B-15 on your Project Disk to HTML using the filename "Spills" and the title "Oil Spills." Edit the resulting Web page as necessary, apply a theme, and make other appropriate changes. Create a hyperlink to return to the Fox home page. Save your changes, click Yes to overwrite the changes, and then close the file. Close Excel without saving changes.

f. Convert the PowerPoint presentation IE5 B-16 on your Project Disk to a set of HTML documents with the filename "Prevention" and the title "Prevention Presentation." Create a hyperlink to return to the Fox home page. Save your changes and then close PowerPoint.

g. Format and test the hyperlinks between pages in your Web publication, and then test them in Internet Explorer. If necessary, delete and reapply the bullets on the Fox home page and reapply the theme. Then save the Fox Home file.

h. Print the first page of each of your Web pages using Internet Explorer, then close Internet Explorer and Word.

▶ Visual Workshop

You are an employee at the Lakeview Café. The manager wants to post information about the restaurant's specials on the restaurant's Web site. Use the Left-aligned Column Web page template in Word to create the café's specials page shown in Figure B-19. Sketch what a publication for this restaurant should look like, and then create an appropriate home page to accompany the specials page with a link to open it. Create at least two other associated Web pages by creating files in Office programs and then converting them to HTML and formatting them. Finally, add links between your pages. Print the first page of each of your Web pages using Internet Explorer. (*Hint:* The graphic is included in the Web page template.)

FIGURE B-19

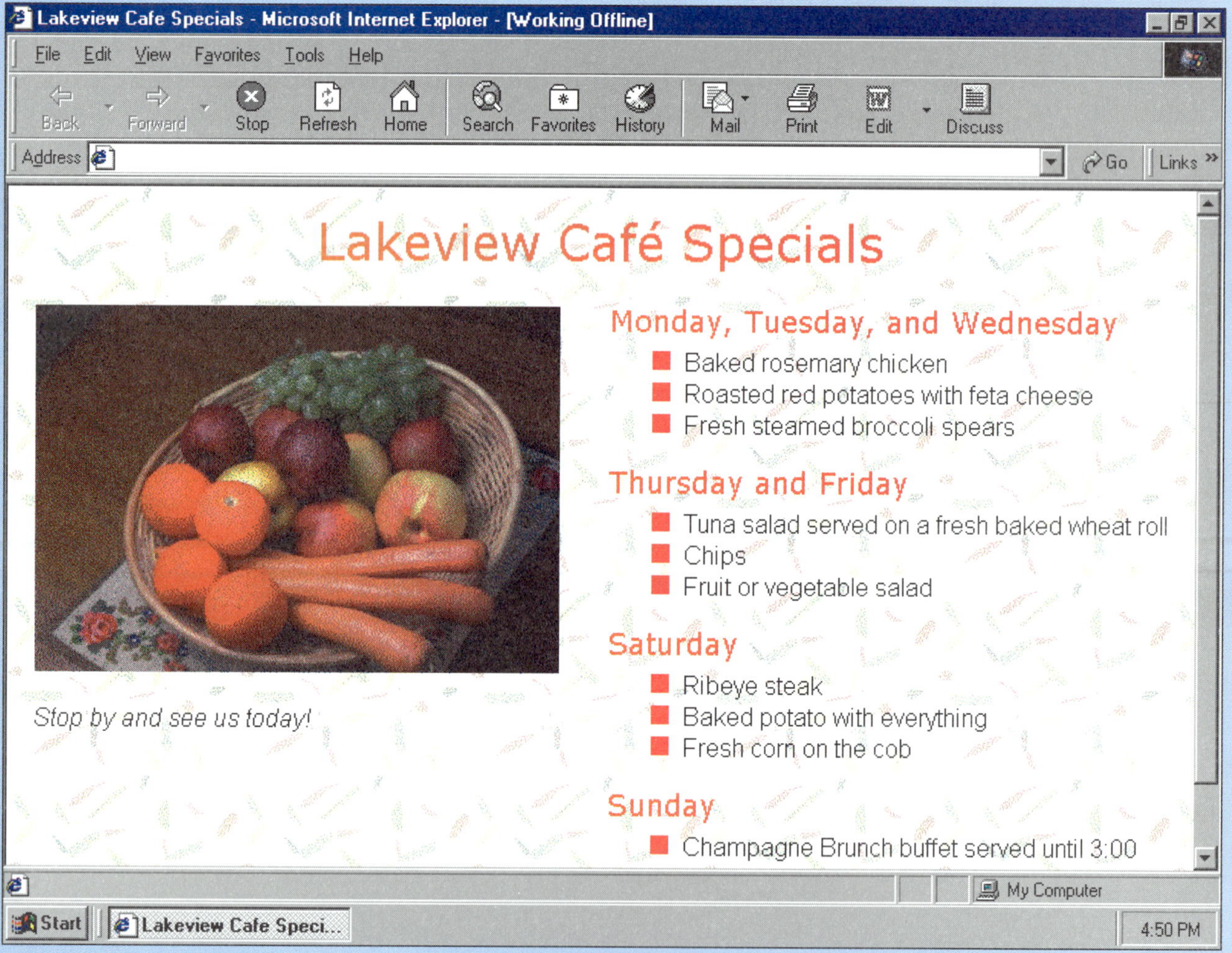

Internet

Glossary

Absolute link A link that contains a fixed address; used when you don't want the link's address to change.

Address bar The bar that indicates the address of the Web page currently opened in the Web browser window.

Computer network Two or more connected computers that can share information and resources.

Crawl The process by which a Web search engine methodically catalogs the entire Internet to create huge databases with links to Web pages and their URLs.

Document window See *Web page area.*

Dynamic HTML page A method of linking a Web page to the original database file that was used to create it.

Explorer Search bar The frame that opens in the left pane and contains the Search Assistant when you use Internet Explorer's search feature.

Favorites list A list of frequently visited Web pages that you can open by clicking a link in the list.

FrontPage Express (FrontPage) A program that is included as part of the Internet Explorer 5 suite specifically designed for Web page production. It provides tools for creating new Web pages and editing existing ones.

Hits The result of an Internet search that, when clicked, opens a Web page or category.

Home page The first page that opens every time you start Internet Explorer.

Hyperlinks Web pages that contain highlighted words, phrases, or graphics that open other Web pages when clicked. Also known as *Links.*

Hypertext Markup Language (HTML) The language used to describe the content and format of Web pages.

Internet A communications system that connects computers and computer networks located around the world using telephone lines, cables, satellites, and other telecommunications media.

Internet Explorer 5 A popular browser from Microsoft that comes with Microsoft Office 2000.

Intranet A computer network that connects computers in a local area only, such as computers in a company's office.

Links See *Hyperlinks.*

Menu bar The bar beneath the title bar that lists the menus that contain the program's commands.

Mosaic The first graphical Web browser.

NetMeeting An Internet Explorer suite component that enables you to set up audio and video links to people at different locations for a live discussion.

Outlook Express An Internet Explorer suite component that allows you to read and send e-mail messages as well as read and post messages in newsgroups (discussions organized around specific topics).

Personal Web Server An Internet Explorer suite component that lets you use your personal computer to host a Web site.

Publish The process of placing Web pages on an intranet or the Web so people can access them using a Web browser.

Relative link A link that gives another page's address in relation to the current page.

Scroll box A movable box in the scroll bar that you drag to move around in a Web page.

Search Assistant A search feature that lists search options for finding Web pages, people, businesses, previous searches, or maps.

Search engine An Internet site that lets you enter a keyword or phrase describing the information you want to find and then provides you with a list of related Web sites.

Static HTML page A Web page that contains the current information in an Access database table that you are converting to a Web page.

Status bar A bar located at the bottom of the Web browser window that displays information about your connection progress whenever you open a new Web page, notifies you when you connect to another Web site, and identifies the percentage of information transferred from the Web server to your browser. It also displays the Web addresses of any links on the Web page when you move your mouse pointer over them.

Status indicator The Internet Explorer logo on the toolbar that animates while a new Web page loads.

Surfing The process of using the Web and navigating to new Web pages and sites.

Tags The codes that HTML places around all the elements in a Web document that describe how they should appear when viewed using a Web browser.

Title bar The bar at the top of the window that indicates the name of the program and the name of the Web page currently displayed in the Web browser window.

Toolbar A bar that contains buttons that give you quick access to the most frequently used commands, such as moving from one Web page to another, printing Web pages, and searching for information on the Internet.

Uniform Resource Locator (URL) A Web page's address.

Vertical scroll bar A scroll bar that allows you to move the current Web page up or down in the Web browser window.

Web browsers Software programs used to access and open Web pages.

Web page area The specific area where the current Web page appears.

Web publication A group of associated Web pages focusing on a particular theme or topic.

Windows Media Player An Internet Explorer suite component that lets you listen to and/or view live and prerecorded sounds, images, and videos.

World Wide Web (Web or **WWW)** A part of the Internet containing Web pages that are linked together.

Index

Index

W